The
SHEPHERD'S
VIEW

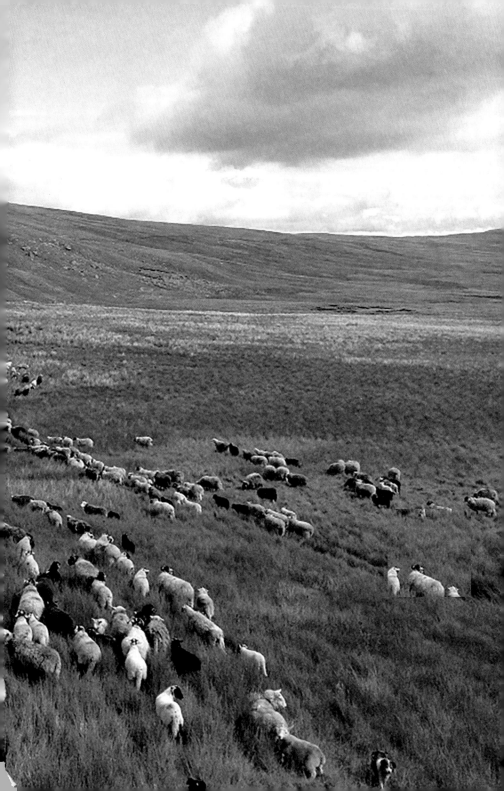

ALSO BY JAMES REBANKS

The Shepherd's Life:
Modern Dispatches from an Ancient Landscape

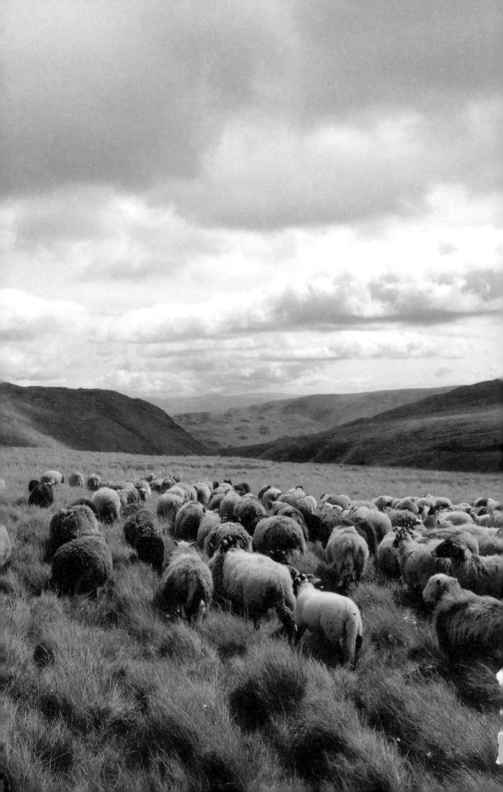

The
SHEPHERD'S VIEW

Modern Photographs from an Ancient Landscape

JAMES REBANKS

FLATIRON
BOOKS
NEW YORK

Photographs appearing on pp. 80, 82, 83, and 85 by Joseph Hardman, courtesy of Lakeland Life and Industry, Lakeland Arts Trust, Kendal; photographs appearing on pp. 70 and 73 © Michael Eleftheriader; all other photographs © James Rebanks.

Cover photograph © James Rebanks
Cover design by Karen Horton, based on original
UK cover design by Clare Skeats
Book design by Michelle McMillian

www.flatironbooks.com

The Library of Congress Cataloging-in-Publication Data
is available upon request.

ISBN 978-1-250-10336-9 (paper over board)
ISBN 978-1-250-10337-6 (ebook)

Originally published in the UK, in slightly different form,
as *The Illustrated Herdwick Shepherd*

Our books may be purchased in bulk for promotional, educational, or business use. Please contact your local bookseller or the Macmillan Corporate and Premium Sales Department at 800-221-7945, extension 5442, or by e-mail at MacmillanSpecialMarkets@macmillan.com.

First U.S. Edition: October 2016

10 9 8 7 6 5 4 3 2 1

*For the men and women who
make this landscape what it is.*

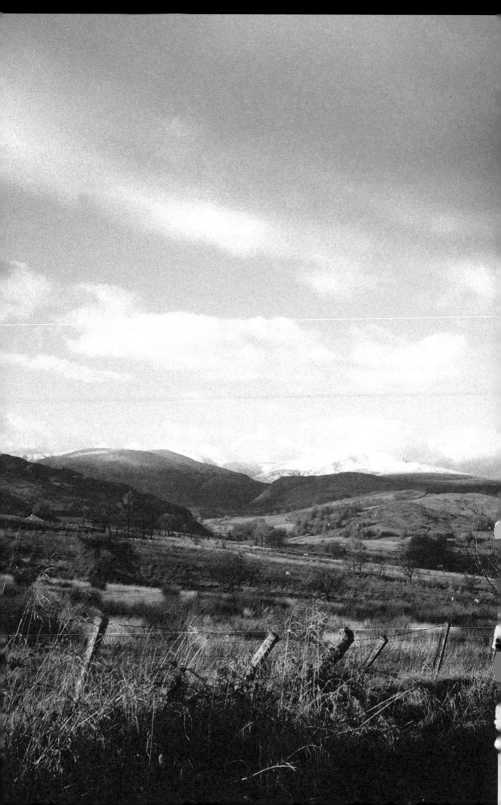

I am the luckiest man alive, because I get to live and work in the most beautiful place on earth: Matterdale in the English Lake District.

When I was a child we didn't really go anywhere, except for a week on the Isle of Man when I was about ten years old, and I never left Britain until I was twenty.

Even now, years later, the best bit of any travelling is coming home.

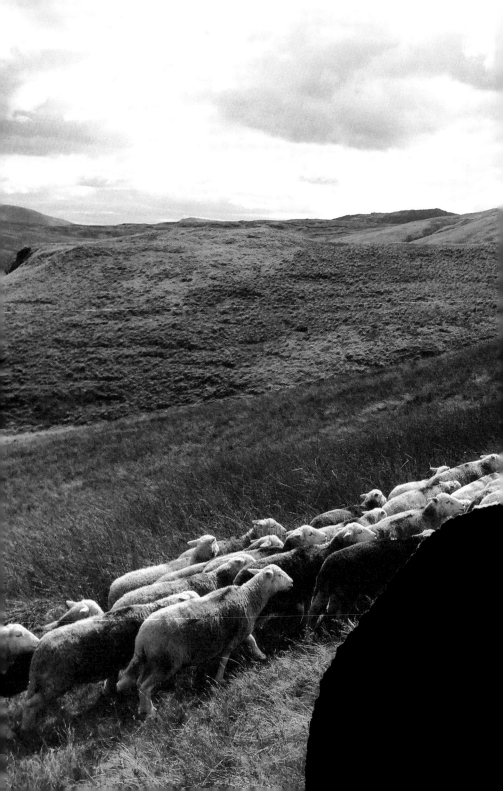

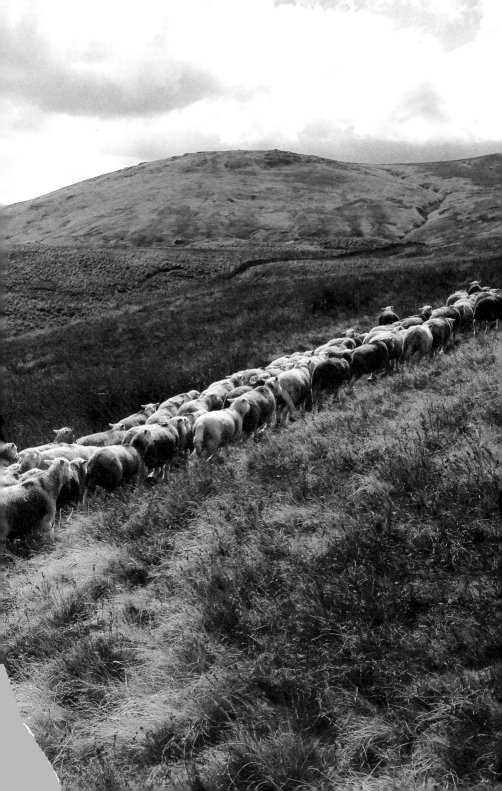

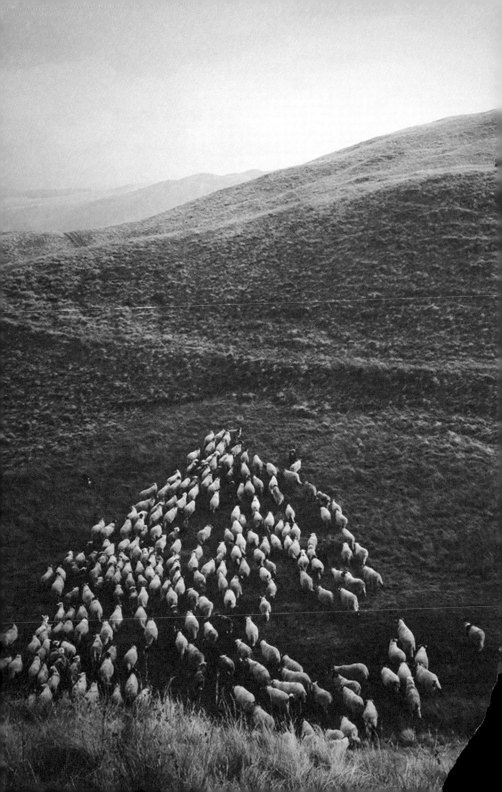

Setting the Scene

I live and work in the English Lake District, a tiny little chunk of Northwest England just beneath the Scottish border. It doesn't have the biggest mountains in the world, or the largest lakes, or the most spectacular waterfalls, or even the most amazing creatures, and it isn't very wild.

But it is one of the most important landscapes on earth, and it became important by an accident of history.

Until the mid-eighteenth century, ours was a surprisingly difficult place to get to. You had to pass over mountains or moorland, or even over the sands of an estuary between tides. So an older way of life survived here, protected by poverty and isolation.

Then, with the growing prosperity of Britain as a trading and industrial nation, new roads in were built, and the old clashed with the new. Suddenly this place became a battleground between the forces of change in the name of progress and other voices that said its valleys, lakes, and small farms should be conserved and protected from industry and development. The world had gotten smaller, and our lands were now just an hour or two north by carriage, and later by train or car, from the birthplace of the industrial revolution, Lancashire. It could all have been swept away, but it wasn't.

Writers, artists, and thinkers flooded into our landscape and found in it a counterpoint to everything that worried them about the emerging modern world and what William Blake called its "dark satanic mills."

For the first time people formulated arguments for conservation, for a public interest in protecting endangered places—arguments that are now familiar to everyone around the world.

The Lake District became over time the most written-about landscape in English literature. Most influential amongst these writers were the poets William Wordsworth and Samuel Taylor Coleridge, but many others came, too. They defined what we think of as beautiful in nature and craft around the world, promoting an eye-pleasing combination of the natural and manmade. A generation or two before that, mountains were thought to be menacing and ugly, but suddenly fashions changed and mountain valleys with pretty lakes were all the rage.

Wordsworth summed up what many of these artists felt when he wrote that this landscape was "a sort of national property in which every man has a right and interest who has an eye to perceive and a heart to enjoy."

Those were radical, world-changing words in 1810, the first published call anywhere for something like a national park.

He also described the region as a "perfect republic of shepherds," a place where aristocratic elites had little power over the working people who had secured legal tenure to their land. The people working on the land and shaping it were deemed to matter.

A generation later, other wealthy individuals bought many of the small farms to protect them from change and development. Most famously, Beatrix Potter invested the proceeds from her bestselling children's books about Peter Rabbit and his friends in this way.

Potter and other benefactors left these farms and their hefted flocks of fell sheep ("hefted" means sheep being tied to a part of the mountain or moorland by a sense of belonging taught by their mothers, despite the mountains being unfenced "common land") to the National Trust to be protected and sustained for the good of the nation.

So this is a national park, but not the kind that an American might recognize. Unlike Yellowstone or Yosemite, it isn't a wilderness, and it doesn't belong to the government. It has instead a complicated and messy English tapestry of ownership.

The National Trust is a charity that protects some things in our landscapes or towns. It doesn't own all or even most of the land, just some small special bits within it. Farming families, like us, own other bits of it and are its stewards.

It is a national park because it is a landscape molded by being farmed, because it inspired important ideas about nature, and because it was one of the birthplaces of the worldwide conservation movement.

The thirteen valleys of the Lake District cover just 885 square miles, and contain more than two hundred fells, sixteen lakes, and countless tarns (think a pond on a mountain). It is home to more than forty thousand people, and every inch of its protected landscape tells a story about how people have lived in it for ten thousand years (and farmed it for five thousand). Today sixteen million people a year visit the Lake District.

It is also the largest area of common land in Western Europe, a unique preservation of a way of farming once experienced everywhere, until land was enclosed and put under the ownership of individuals, for their sole use, instead of existing for communities. On our common land survives an ancient farming system and breeds of sheep that make it work. All of this survives in the midst of crowded modern Britain and a world in constant flux.

When English people dream of a rural arcadia, they usually dream of our landscape.

My family is simply one of two hundred to three hundred such families who still live and farm this land.

The unique history of this place made for a particular kind of people. The fells and long, wet, cold winters make people here tough and intolerant of nonsense. The people are deeply rooted on their land, and families go back many generations alongside each other. The common land system means we have to work together as shepherds. We have a strong ethical code based on collaboration, honoring other people's property and rights, and acting decently.

My shepherding life is not unique, but the product of an ancient legacy that still is very much alive. I hope it lives for many generations to come.

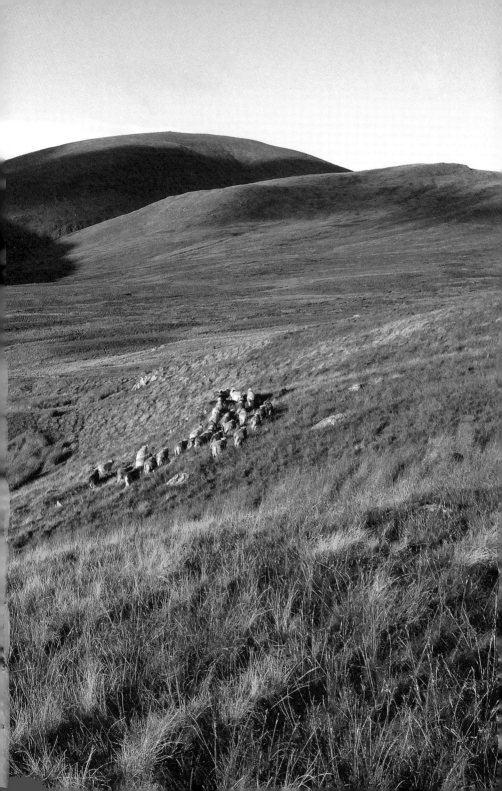

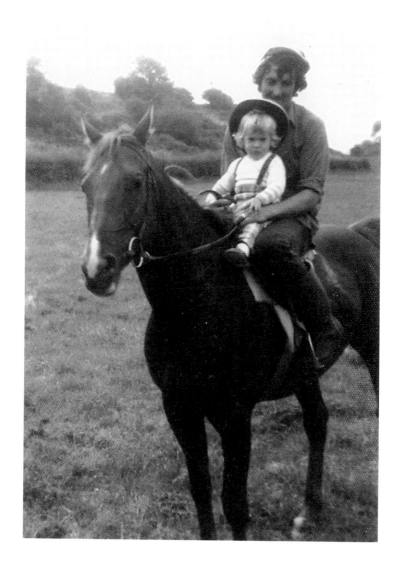

BEGINNING

I'm running down the concrete path that leads from our council house to the gate on the road, because I heard Dad get home from the farm on his tractor. I'm wearing a cowboy outfit, with two holsters at the hips, and pink dungarees, and I have blond wavy hair (forgive me, it is 1978). I am four years old. As I get halfway, the gate hinges screech open. I run into his legs and he throws me in the air. He carries me over his shoulder back to the house and asks me how the pet lambs are doing. I tell him they are doing fine, that Mum and I fed them a little while ago, that they nearly knocked me over, they are getting so strong.

This is my first memory.

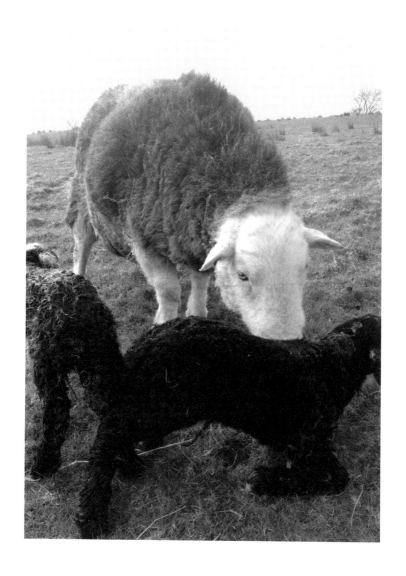

BETTY AND LETTUCE

My pet lambs were two runty orphans that lived in a pen built out of rabbit wire and were fed out of old lemonade bottles in our back garden. Like most pet lambs, they were a bit potbellied.

Betty and Lettuce grew up to be ewes in the flock. I was allowed to sell their lambs each year and keep the money for my savings. But as I got older, my interest changed to our finest pedigree sheep and my ambitions switched to breeding and selling tups (the males we sold each autumn to other flocks for high prices). That was where the real action was, and how you earned the respect of the other shepherds. By the time I was fifteen nothing else mattered much: I did a lot of the work on my father's and grandfather's flock, and was counted as one of the men when we prepared them for sale and then sold them.

I've been sheep-nuts ever since, though I also had a calf at the farm called Goldilocks. It was as small as me, but grew and grew until it towered over me and weighed about a ton.

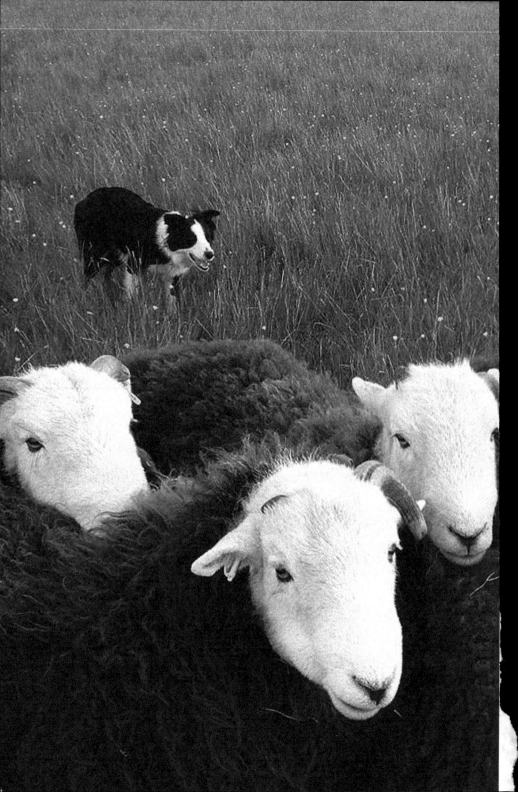

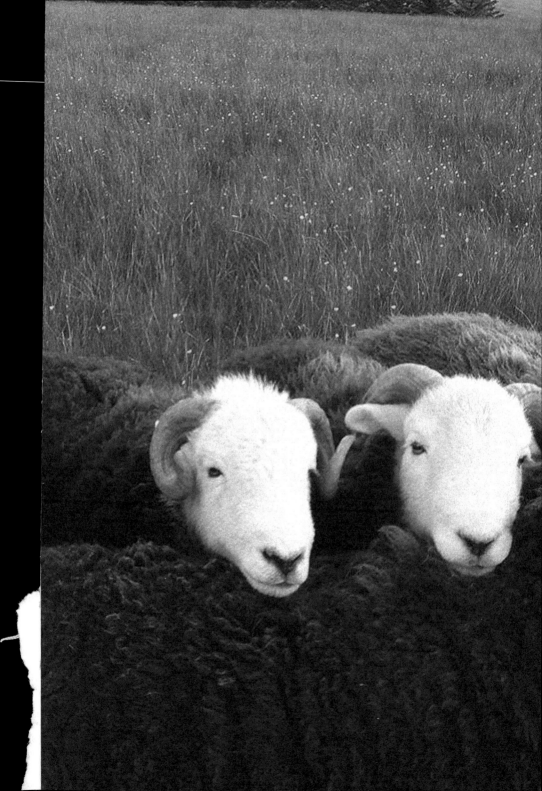

HOW TO SPEAK SHEPHERD

When I was a kid, my cousins from southern England would come to stay, and they hadn't a clue what my dad was saying. We'd be working in a field, gathering some sheep, and he'd shout something like "Git yursel ower't yat and turn them yows down't lonnin." Throw in a bit of wind and the fact he was running across a field and shouting, and maybe it really wasn't clear to the ear. The cousins would shrug in complete bafflement.

Shepherding in this landscape has its own dialect that flows from the unique work that people here do. The writers who pitched up in the eighteenth and nineteenth centuries found a people that didn't sound like they were English; they sounded more like survivors of the Viking world of which they were once a part. Today we "switch codes" between our own dialect and a northern version of the Queen's English, depending on who we are talking to. What follows is a taste of our dialect:

Git: Go.

Yursel: Yourself.

Ower: Over.

Yat: Gate. Shut it behind you.

Yows: Ewes. If you haven't got any, you are maybe not so local.

Lonnin: Lane.

Tip: Ram. You live in West Cumbria.

Tup: Ram. You live somewhere else in Cumbria.

How's t' ga'an on?: Roughly translates as "How are you doing?" Usually said in a fairly noncommittal way because the asker doesn't care that much. A conversation opener.

Alreet: All right. When someone says "How's t' ga'an on?," Cumbrian etiquette requires you to say "Alreet" (even if you are at death's door or have a leg hanging off). It is considered fairly pathetic to reply in the negative, as in, "Actually I'm feeling under the weather." Technically you are always "alreet."

Alreet, luv?: Roughly translates as "You look ill, darling. Please don't die and leave me, as there is a lot of work to do and I don't even know how to work the kettle."

Ga'an yam: Roughly translates as "going home." I tried this in Norway and they understood perfectly. If you are at someone's house and the host says to their partner, "When r' theez sooners ga'an yam?," it is not good.

Sooner: Insult. Used as in "This fella is a sooner," the implication being that the man in question would "sooner watch the Jeremy Kyle show and eat crisps on the sofa than do a day's work."

Yew/yewers: Roughly translates as "you" or "it's yours." Used as in "That yow is yewers, it dun't belong to me."

Thine: Yewers, not mine.

Buke: Cumbrian for "book." There are only two, and they aren't written by Wordsworth or Coleridge. The "buke" is either *The Shepherd's Guide,* which gives the different flock marks, or the flock book, which captures the breeding of the sheep. Very few other books matter.

I's not being funny, but...: Used in advance of some withering insult or personality deconstruction, as in "I'm not being funny or owt, but you look hellish."

Twining: Still can't believe that this isn't used everywhere. Roughly translates as "moaning." Used as a verb, as in "Stop yewer bloody twining and get on with it."

Iz that t' fashion?: Something you say to young people to make them feel insecure about their dress sense.

Ratching bugger: Sheep, dog, or man that strays somewhere it shouldn't be.

Tek care lambs ont' road: Road sign used locally. Means "Slow down your car, because this isn't Daytona and if you don't you will crash into my sheep round the next corner."

Mowdy: A mole. Small velvety-skinned creature that burrows under the ground and hunts worms viciously. Very likely from the OldNorse "mowdywarp." I have no idea what Vikings were doing with moles.

They say it takes light eight minutes to travel from the sun to the earth, and it is worth the journey because when it lights up this valley it takes your breath away.

The sun throws one finger at a time over the fell and into the darkness of the valley floor. It casts long shadows through the oak trees in the dykes, and the tree shadows walk across the fields.

The south-facing grass glows an early-morning green. Some lambs race along the fence by the house.

I can't sleep again now.

The fields are calling me out.

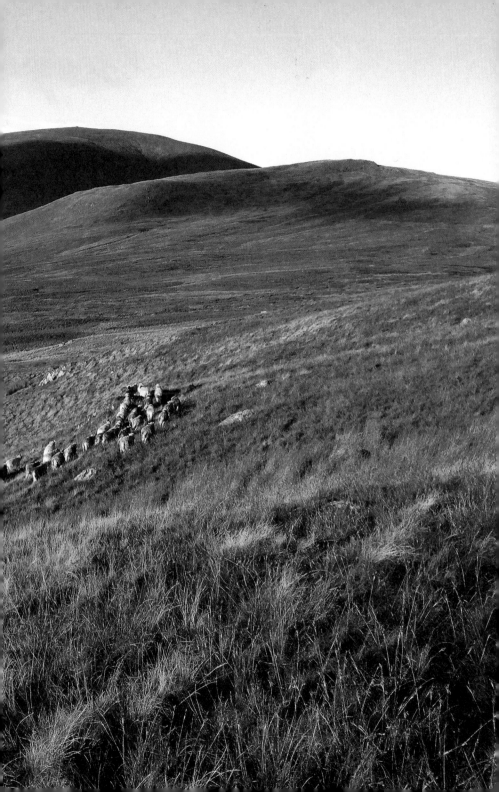

Foreigner: Not from this valley, possibly from as far afield as Penrith. To be distrusted; unlikely to be useful.

Incomer: Colonist from beyond Shap Fell. Almost certainly useless.

Supper: Evening meal.

Tea: Copious amounts of cake, washed down with a gallon of milky tea at midafternoon.

Dinner: Not a posh meal at 8 p.m. Midday meal.

Dinner party: Unlikely.

Thuz done alreet: Ultimate compliment. Only uttered when someone wins a Nobel Prize, or something of real importance like the most prestigious sheep show here, Eskdale Show.

Thuz wrang: You are not right.

Thuz not reet: You are very wrong.

Thuz a long way frae reet: You won't be asked to do this again. You are an idiot.

I'm cum to keep ya reet: I'm going to hang about whilst you do this job and tell you (and anyone else who will listen) how badly you are doing it.

All of the above should be shouted aggressively, as if it's windy, even if it isn't.

LEARNING TO BE (UN)COOL

When I was seventeen I learnt to drive, and it was agreed that I should spend my savings on a car. That's what all the cool lads did, and it seemed to help you get a girlfriend. But I went to an auction and fell in love with one of the best tups I've ever seen.

He was a beautiful sheep, proud and stylish and everything I thought our flock needed. He had incredible bone (thick, chunky legs) and a lot of swagger. We were in Kelso, in the Scottish Borders, at the tup (ram) sales. This is one of the largest sheep fairs in Europe, maybe the world. Thousands of tups are sold in one day in a dozen or so different sale rings, all at the end of a large tent full of some of the finest sheep you'll ever see. Because all the sale rings operate simultaneously, tups from the great flocks can be sold at the same time, which means we might try and fail to win a tup in one ring while missing out on a potential purchase in another. This was all much worse before mobile phones. That year I was sent to one ring where I saw the tup I wanted up for sale.

I bought him for twenty-two hundred guineas (a guinea is one pound and five pence: we always make our sales in guineas instead of pounds; farmers are keeping the old currency alive), emptying my savings account of my "car fund." My dad seemed slightly shocked I'd spent so much, but I think he was rather proud of my financial priorities. When word got around about it, it enhanced my shepherding street cred: I was clearly a lad who meant business. For the next few years I had to borrow my dad's car to go anywhere, and I had no luck getting a girlfriend, but I wasn't that bothered, because I had a great tup.

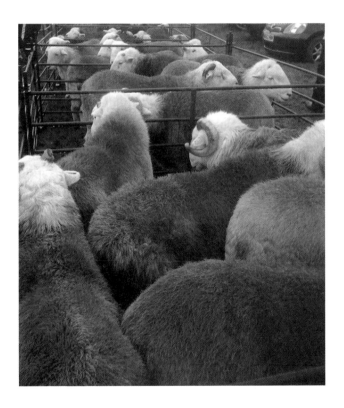

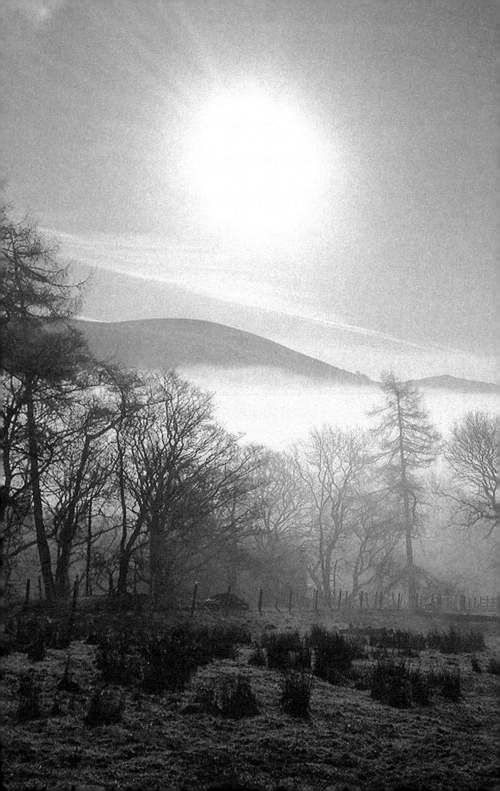

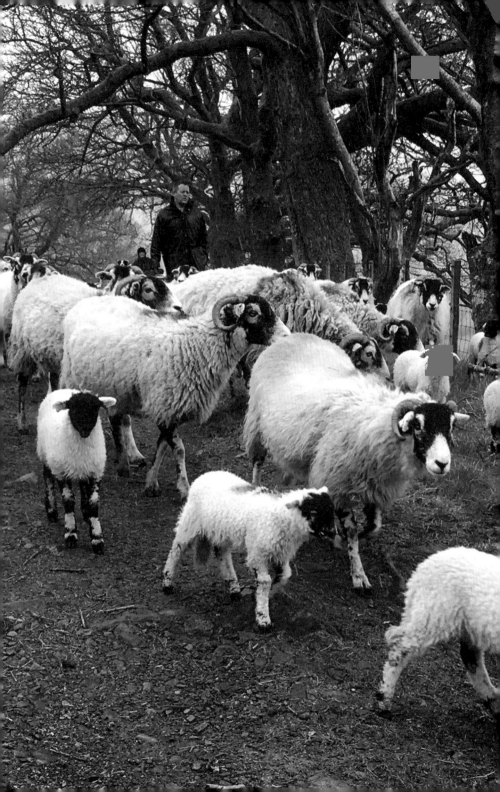

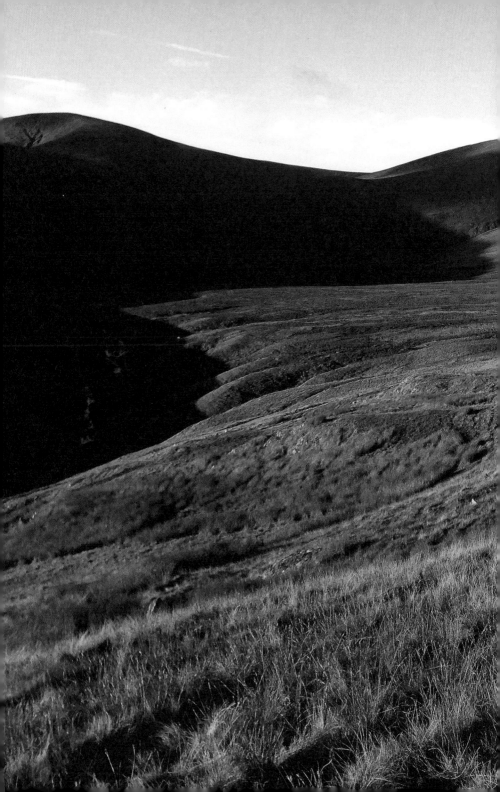

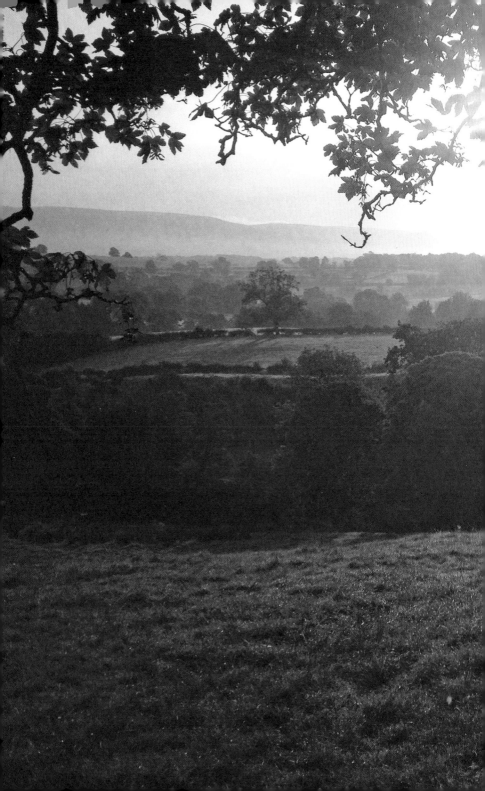

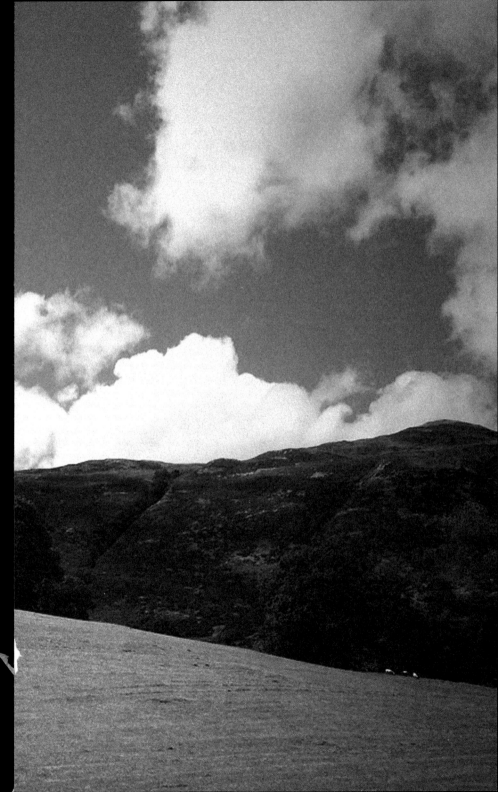

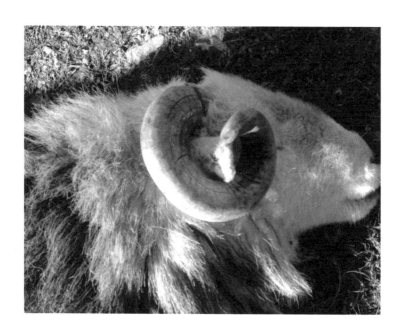

DON'T MENTION THE
DEAD SHEEP

For every day of beauty there are innumerable days of fury and storms, days of heartache at the death of one of my best tups, moments of blood, afterbirth, and shit. I don't tend to record these; there aren't many photos of the weather that we live and work in through the winter months. No one really wants to see pictures of dead sheep, and there are only so many pictures you can take of rain or mud. Something in your brain wants to censor it and focus on the beautiful sunset that follows. And of course there are practical reasons: on wet, windy, and rainy days, it is harder to take a picture. The bad weather puts the pressure on to feed and look after the sheep more quickly than usual.

We joke that we have nine months of rain and three months of snow, and it is true that, for all its beauty and character, this landscape often throws the weather in our faces, burning the skin and swelling the hands. So I try, when I can, to take pictures of the rainy days, the snowy days, the grey days. I am always dreaming, then, of getting warm by the fire.

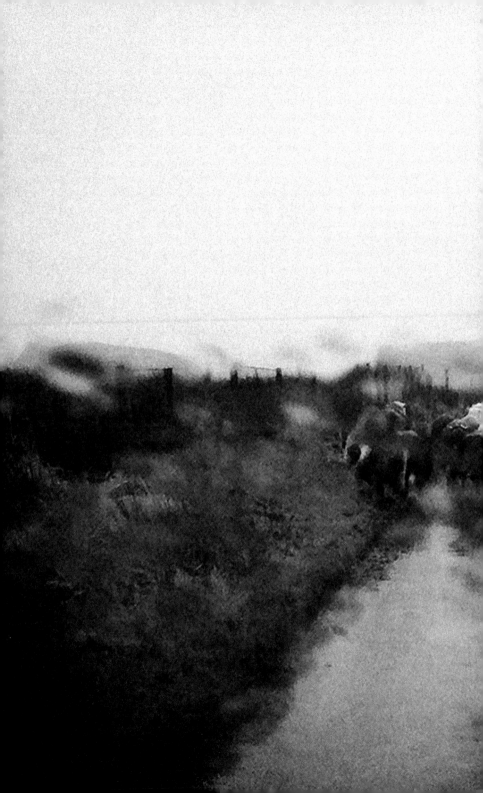

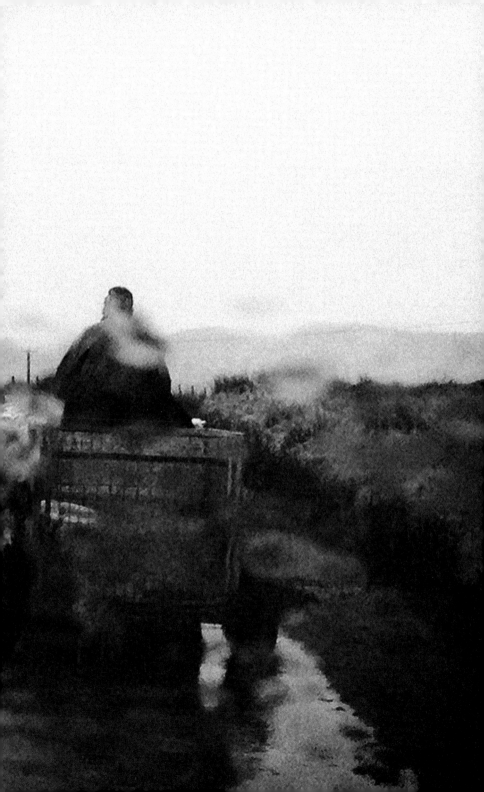

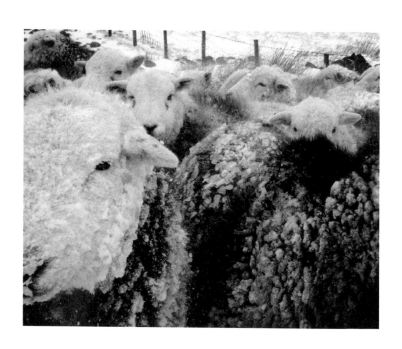

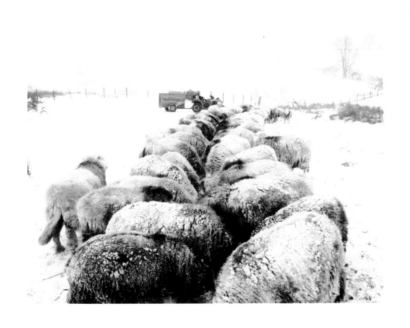

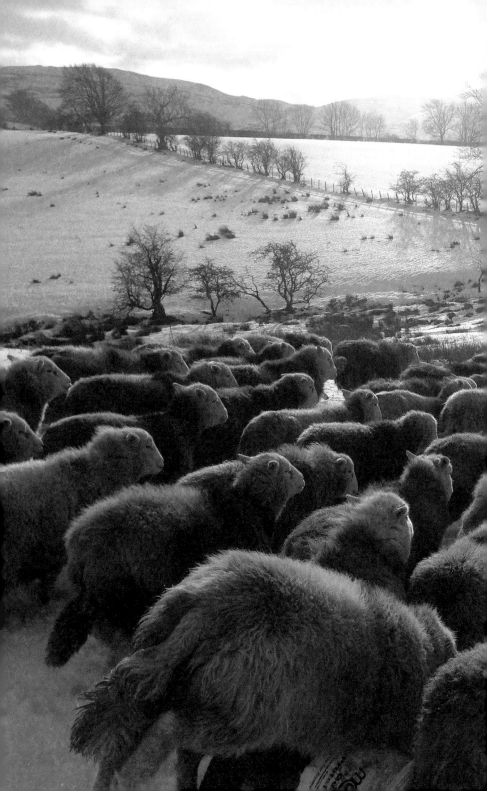

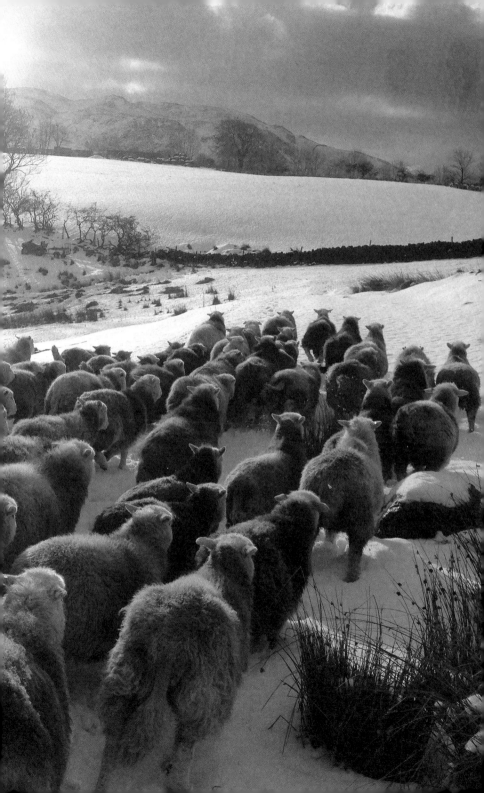

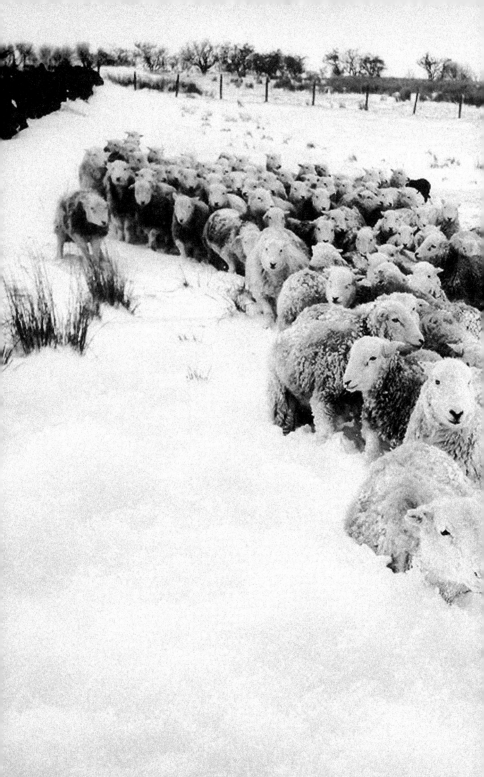

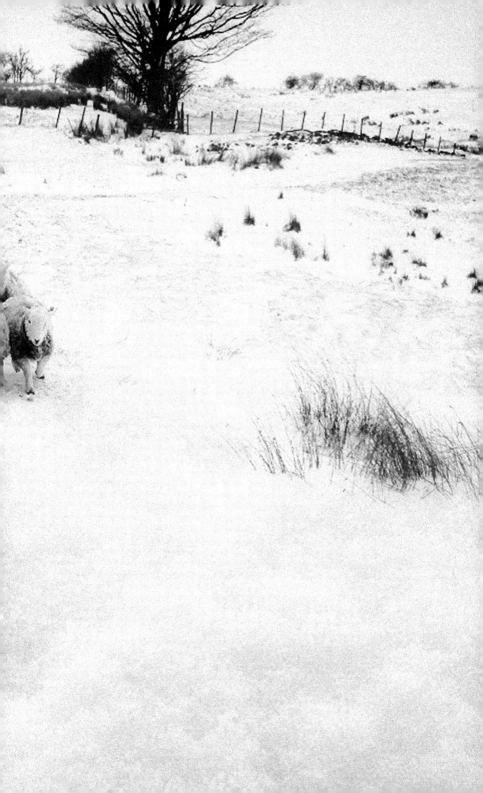

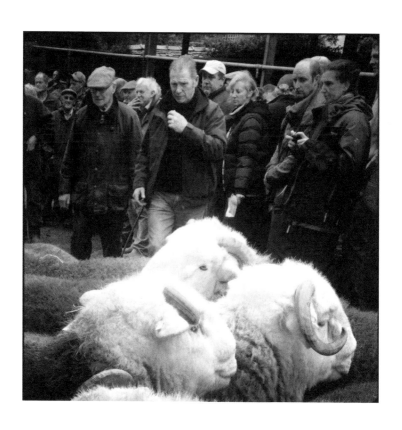

INTRODUCTION
TO SHEEP SHOWS

Shepherding isn't just about looking after the sheep, or standing on biblical hillsides looking for twinkly stars; it is about the breeding sheep that are to be sold.

My job as a shepherd is to look after my stock and their lambs so well that I have surplus of lambs and ewes to sell each autumn (by producing and keeping alive more sheep than I need to maintain the number in my flock). Many of these spare sheep are sold to other shepherds in the autumn sales, in September and October, to bolster their flocks with new genes. Lots are sold to the lowland farmers who use the mountains as a nursery for their commercial flocks.

But the key question is why do they want to buy my sheep, rather than those raised by any one of hundreds of other shepherds?

As with any other thing for sale, I need my sheep to seem like they are better than everyone else's, worth the attention and money it will take to buy them. A long time ago, the shepherds here became deeply competitive with their flocks. When they gathered the fells in the autumn, they did what shepherds do, and started to comment on each other's sheep.

"Joseph's are bigger than yours."

"Isaac's live longer because they have better teeth."

"Anthony's produce tastier meat."

"Mine are tougher and survived the snow better in the winter; yours might be more productive, but I have more left than you."

And because a flock of sheep only needs a small number of tups (they can each mate a hundred or more females), the natural way to improve a flock or add characteristics is to buy a tup carrying the genetic qualities you admire or need. So the handful of tups have a value that far exceeds that of a normal sheep; they are, we say, "half the flock," literally worth half the value of the flock.

So the flocks are watched very carefully for subtle little qualities that another shepherd might require in his own flock. This standing, looking, and talking about the sheep morphed over time into formal competitions called shepherds' meets, in which sheep were judged based on everything from the quality of the teeth to the wool to the finer breed points. A respected shepherd from another valley would be asked to come and judge. And the bragging rights in the valley were earned by winning the shepherds' meet and having the champion sheep in the dale.

Fast-forward many centuries, and we still have shepherds' meets. What we do at a meet might seem odd to anyone who doesn't understand its roots or its functions, not least because the prize money is trivial, but these things matter as much today as they did a century ago.

When I take my sheep to the sales, I want my pen to be crowded with other shepherds who have been impressed by my sheep at the shepherds' meet and come when it counts at the sales to spend their money on them.

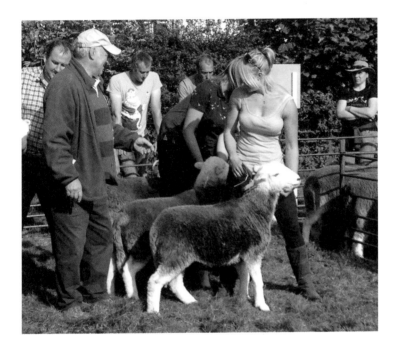

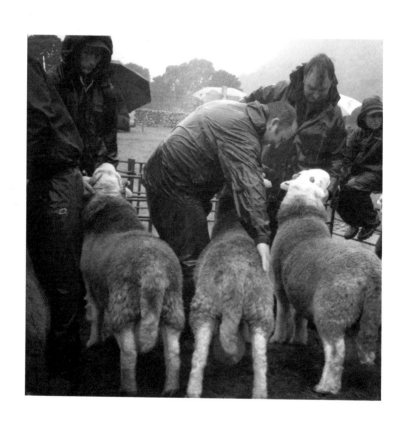

BEAUTY TREATMENTS, PART 1: HERDWICK

We once moved house while I was at a sheep sale. I didn't know anything about it until my wife called to tell me we had moved and that when I came home I should go to the new house.

"But who moved everything?"

"Removal men, you idiot. I hope you made good prices with your sheep, because you're paying them."

Doing well in the autumn shows, winning prizes, catching the eye of other shepherds, helps to showcase the quality of your flock, which helps you to sell your sheep for higher prices in the autumn sales. So the keenest shepherds become artists at making their sheep beautiful and turning them out in peak condition.

Herdwicks are a hardy breed, bred by very practical folk, so the preparations for shows and sales are minimal. Some shepherds bring them straight from the field and do a quick wash in the show pens, though they are subjected to some tut-tutting for not having done this the day before.

But most of us shepherds still have our beauty rituals for the sheep. We would no more send a sheep to a show or sale in its natural condition than Dolly Parton would go out without her makeup.

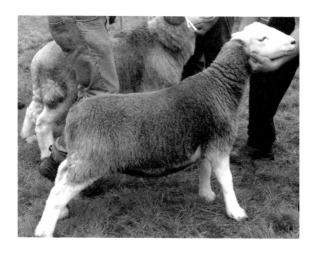

THE WEEK BEFORE THE SHOW OR SALE

Bring sheep into the barn or pen. One shepherd should hold the sheep while the other applies the "Herdwick Show Red" to its back. Herdwick Show Red is a kind of raddle (a coloured powder mixed with water or oil that is applied to a tup's chest, so that when he mates with a ewe we know she has been mated). It replicates the colour of the iron ore rust in the fell sides. It has been applied for so long we don't exactly know why we do it. The Herdwick Show Red is mixed with a dash of water or oil to make a sticky paste. Then you cover both your hands in it and pull them towards your body, from the sheep's neck to its tail. If the sheep is a "good colour" (i.e., its fleece is a lovely slatey blue) then you don't need to apply much, just a two-hands'-width stripe along the top of the back. If it is a whiter-fleeced sheep, then you can plaster it on in a vain attempt to hide this flaw. It is traditional to get covered in raddle yourself, until you look like a mass murderer covered in dried blood.

THE DAY BEFORE THE SHOW OR SALE

Bring sheep into the barn or pen. One person should hold the sheep tight under the chin, and the other wash the white heads and legs with soapy water, leaving the wool and redded bits alone. Then let the sheep go and marvel at how idiotic they can be as they rub their white bits on their raddled bits and defeat the point of the whole washing exercise by going out with heads and legs a smudgy red.

SHOW OR SALE DAY

Bring sheep into the pen, add final touches of raddle, and wash heads and legs again with warm soapy water. Then curse like a trooper when you get to the auction or show field and discover the sheep have all rubbed on each other and are smudgy red again. Wash heads and legs repeatedly, with a damp cloth, throughout the day. Make a resolution not to red your sheep next year. (Next year you will ignore this resolution and repeat the whole process.) The finished article is a sheep with white legs and head—"hoar-frosted," to use the technical term. The legs and head look brighter and more brilliant because they contrast with the redded fleece. To us, a redded Herdwick in peak condition "just looks right."

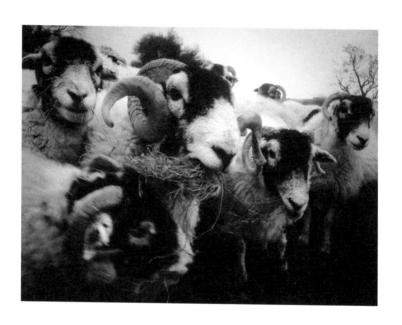

BEAUTY TREATMENTS, PART 2: SWALEDALE

Swaledale breeders do some fairly strange things. Maybe the Pennines, where most of them farm, make people odd. Maybe it is the altitude, or something in the water.

Anyway, here are some instructions in case you ever need to prepare a beautiful Swaledale sheep for a show or sale.

PREVIOUS FOUR WEEKS

Ensure sheep is in good health and blooming by catering to its every dietary and lifestyle whim. Sheep should be not too lean, not too fat, but in good fettle, and, as the old shepherds say, "improving." Inevitably the sheep will get a dirty backside, decide to lose its wool or rub it off, or have some kind of freak accident that cripples it—so consider bringing the sheep into the house to live, making a small pen by your bed so you can keep an eye on it through the night.

Bring sheep into a pen and put it in a holding device (sheep stand still and calm if properly held behind the head in a holding crate, and soon begin to enjoy being pampered). Talk sweetly to the sheep, give it a scratch, and tell it how beautiful it is, until it is relaxed. Then proceed to pluck carefully, with a pair of ladies' eyebrow tweezers, the stray hairs from the sheep's head and legs. (Note: It is important to buy your own tweezers for sheep, rather than simply taking your wife's from the bathroom.) The goal of this "tonsing" is to make the white speckles a perfect unblemished white and the black bits a perfect matt black. If other nosy shepherds arrive in your yard, shout in a loud voice, "I'm not in today, go away" and hide the tweezers. (The first rule of Sheep Club is you do not talk about Sheep Club.) These visiting troublemakers will want to waste about two hours pulling your sheep to bits and telling you why it is not good enough. Though there's always the chance they'll go all quiet and cryptic, suggesting that it might be okay.

FOUR DAYS TO SHOW OR SALE

Take naturally clean-looking sheep and make its fleece a dark peaty colour (mess). Colour water with peat from a secret place on the moors, traditionally one that is quite inaccessible and a complete ball-ache to get to. Keep said peat-extraction source a total secret from other shepherds, on the off chance it is the perfect colour and they sneak in and take some of the peat. Once sheep is a dirty peat colour, let it out to dry and recover its mental equilibrium. At this stage panic is usual, and a lot of head-scratching takes place.

"Is it too black?"

"Have we put enough on?"

"Is it streaky?"

"Have we overdone it?"

THE DAY BEFORE THE SHOW OR SALE

Bring in the peaty, coal-black sheep and wash the legs and head without washing any of the wool clean. This is impossible, so swear a lot, and throw a little tantrum if it makes you feel better. Result should be the white bits sparkling white and contrasting markedly with the darkness of the fleece. Do not use a softening soap to wash, as the facial hair should be hard to the touch. Let sheep off so it can go and find something dirty to rub itself on to frustrate your plans. Do not shoot the sheep

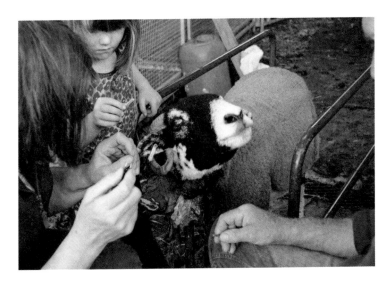

(or yourself) if it rubs itself in engine oil under a tractor: these things happen. If it is being sensible, you can behold it in its prime condition. At this stage you might start a fantasy about how good it is, and how you will win the show and make top price at the sale. If you turn your head on one side at an angle, and squint, sometimes they look better.

SHOW OR SALE DAY

Get up early to see how thoroughly the sheep has messed itself up again. Before loading in trailer, give it a gentle wipe to clean its black and white bits, and do a final few tweaks with your tweezers. At the sale or show deny all knowledge of the cosmetic work described above. You didn't see or do any of these things to your sheep, because your sheep is just naturally beautiful.

If your sheep is a good one and wins the show, or makes a lot of money, you'll feel all this effort was worthwhile; if it doesn't, you will feel an utter fool for wasting several days. Swaledale breeders drink a lot of whisky and beer after shows and sales—perhaps to recover from the stress of all this stuff.

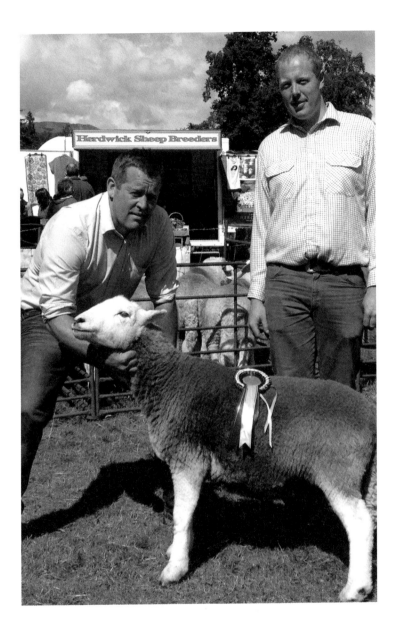

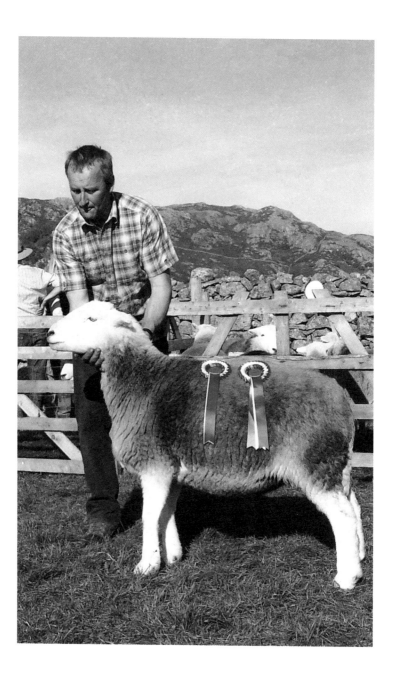

A BEGINNER'S GUIDE TO
JUDGING A HERDWICK

Thousands of years of continuity have made us appreciate great sheep as beautiful (but useful) works of art. Here's a beginner's guide to spotting a good one, starting with the practical stuff.

TEETH

If a sheep can't eat, it will die in the mountains, so shepherds spend a lot of time obsessing about teeth. Teeth matter.

In fact, we even have prizes at shows for the "best mouth." Having short, tough, broad teeth is crucial. There should be no gaps and they should stand straight like a little row of those Portland gravestones for fallen soldiers.

LEGS AND FEET

Fell sheep need to be agile to climb the rocky crags where they usually graze, so sturdy, springy legs and feet are critical. Herdwicks have thick-boned and powerful legs like a Clydesdale horse, on a wide, white "good foot." We like them to be as four-square as possible, with a "leg at each corner."

WOOL

The Lake District fells are often battered by snow and rain, so the sheep need a strong fleece to keep them warm and dry. Because of this, Herdwick wool is perfect for hard-wearing carpets or tweed, but not so good for underpants, as it can be a bit wiry and itchy. Herdwicks used to be woollier than they are now, as wool was once worth much more. The current fashion is to breed them for a shorter, tighter fleece.

BODY

They need to have a long, broad, and meaty body, with a deep barrel chest. They should also have a chunky backside. They need to be stylish with good lines and curves. Think shapely, like Beyoncé.

HARDINESS

Herdwick sheep look as they do because of countless centuries of evolution and selective breeding: if they are too soft they will die in the snow or endless rain; if they are too skinny and goatlike they won't deliver a profit for the farms. Toughness is a key attribute, as is being a good mother and getting your lambs through the bad weather. You can't tell this from looks alone, but it becomes apparent in the spring, and we take notice of the flock the sheep is from.

That's the main practical stuff, and then it gets interesting—or weird, depending on your point of view . . .

CHARACTER AND STYLE

It pays to have sheep that stand out, sheep that have more style and character than the rest. The head should be carried high, with a broad forehead, depth beneath the eye, and a slightly arched Roman nose. The females should have a much more feminine face. In both genders, the body should rise to the shoulder, and then to the head, giving a proud upstanding look. A great sheep carries itself as if it knows it is "someone."

COLOUR

When shepherds talk of colour, they are talking about the overall patterning of a sheep, taking in its grey woollen coat and its head and legs. To have a good colour is to have an eye-pleasing combination of a grey-blue fleece and a distinct "hoar-frosted" white head and legs, with a pronounced contrast between the two. The white bits should be covered in bristly white hair, distinct at the joining places from the woollen areas. Herdwicks are naturally grey-coloured in the fleece, but effectively have "fifty shades of grey" from nearly white to nearly black. All shepherds have their own preferences, but I prefer the sheep to be a slatey blue colour.

STRANGE THINGS THAT MATTER

Keen shepherds obsess about how "clean" the white is on a Herdwick—by which they don't mean washed clean, but naturally devoid of any hint of grey, black, or brown hairs. So they check the ears to ensure they are perfectly white, and behind the legs by parting the wool (in the front armpit). The ears can be too long or at the wrong angle as well: they should be quite short and sharp. There should be no brown on a Herdwick (though at one year old the young sheep have the colour of dark Belgian chocolate—just don't ever use the word "brown" to Herdwick shepherds!). There should be no black spots or speckles on the white bits, but an occasional beauty spot or birthmark is forgiven in an otherwise great sheep. The testicles should be covered in wiry white hair, and there should be two of them. Females should have no horns, or horn buds, at all. Half the males have horns and the other half have none; the half that don't are called "cowed." Having horns or not is irrelevant to their merits, though wild "billy-goat-gruff" horns are frowned upon. Horns should be light coloured and smooth. The eyes should be bright and shiny and healthy looking.

That all sounds easy enough, but last year they asked me to judge one of the most prestigious Herdwick shepherds' meets, at Borrowdale. About 250 almost-perfect Herdwick sheep were presented for judging. I started in the morning and was still judging at 4 p.m. The sheep were stunning examples of shepherding skills, and tiny subjective judgements meant the difference between first and tenth in some classes.

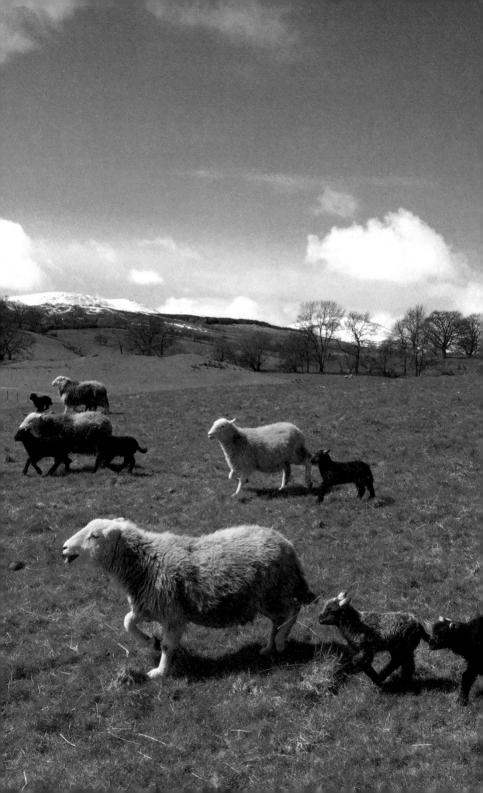

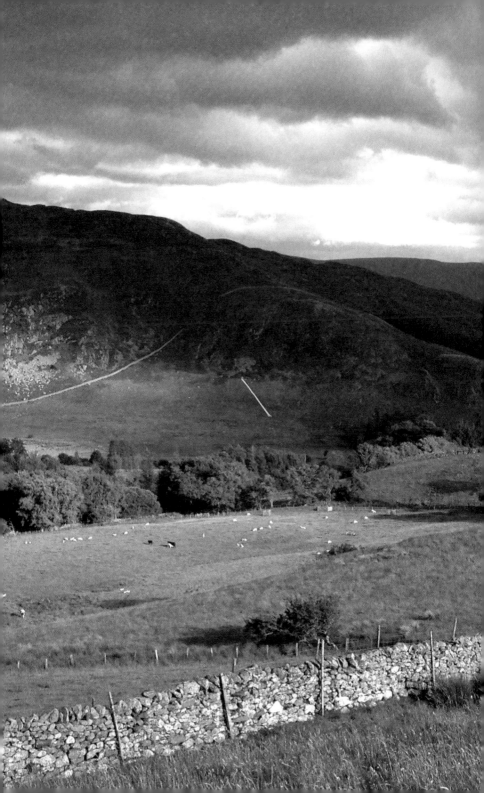

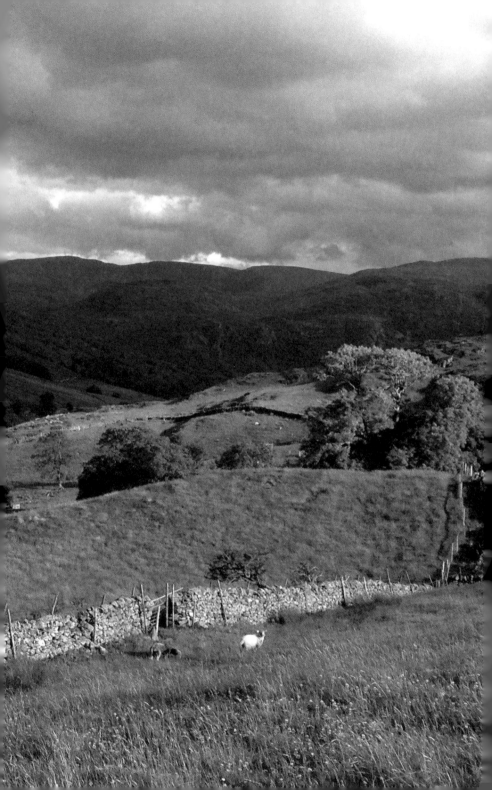

The mornings are sharper now, with heavy dews and the promise of frost.

Racing pigeons pass over the fog and catch the sun like shards of glass. Daddy longlegs breeze across the fields, over tarmac and past houses, draughts gathering them like little crumpled biplanes on the windowsills.

The last of the swallows strengthen their wings against the journey to come, and make off across the heather-raddled shoulder of the fell.

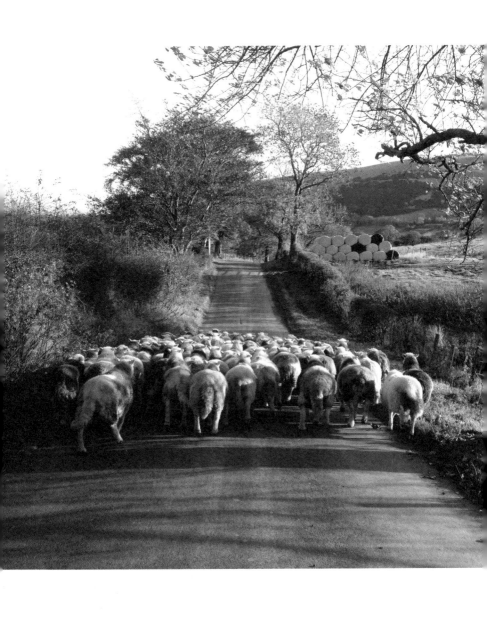

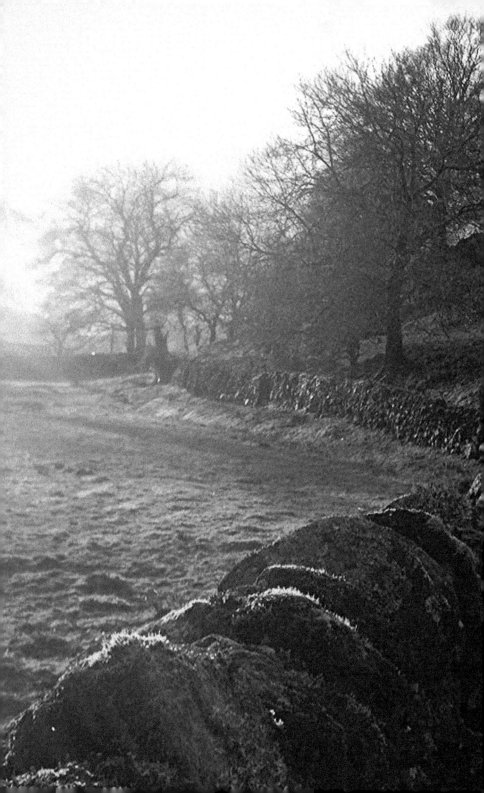

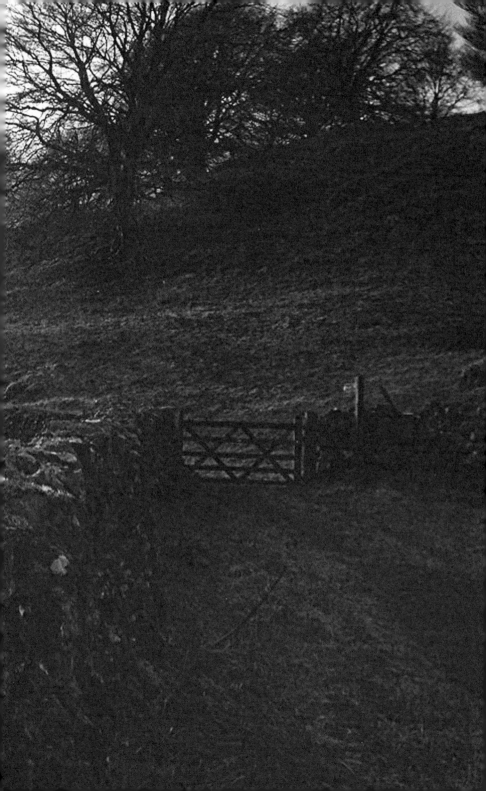

Volume. 1.

THE SHEPHERD'S GUIDE

I'm burning the backside out of my trousers, but I don't yet know it.

Our old farmhouse is so draughty and cold that on winter nights we tend to gravitate around the fire to dry out and get some warmth back into our bones. All around the fire, on the backs of chairs and hanging above me on a clotheshorse, are damp clothes drying out in the heat. So the whole room smells a bit musty and singed, and then I realize that the singed smell is actually my trousers, and I yelp because my arse suddenly feels like it is on fire.

My dad laughs. He is in his armchair, which has pride of place next to the fire, and he is studying the Swaledale flock book. Well, sort of. Actually he falls asleep, mostly, and then grunts back awake and resumes his study from time to time.

The flock book is like a who's who of the pedigree sheep he breeds. It covers the preceding year, recording the pedigrees of the registered sheep and their key achievements. The very finest sheep are photographed at the sales and shows and captured in those pages for generations to come. These flock books have been published each year for a century or more: they are collected by the farming families, and the old ones have a considerable value. When an old shepherd dies, his flock books might be sold, and they can make many hundreds of pounds each, with a full set worth thousands. So Dad is looking through the pictures, trying to work out some breeding quandary or other. It is what old shepherds do on winter nights.

Last year I bought the first-ever Herdwick flock book. It dates from 1920 and cost me a hundred pounds. Some loving past owner had wrapped it in brown greaseproof paper to protect its cover. It lists all the known flocks in 1920, and has a few paragraphs about their history. I love it, this little slice of our world from nearly a century ago, the words attempting to capture the knowledge that shepherds have always carried in their heads. The flocks it describes are nearly all intact today, and farmed by my friends.

The only other book is *The Shepherd's Guide,* a quirky old thing that details every farm's marks and serves as a kind of reference book for shepherds when it comes to identifying stray sheep and returning them to their rightful owners. It is quite a comical book: in order to show the lug marks it has a kind of cartoon sheep with huge ears for each farm. Last week I had to call a farmer from Langdale, an hour's drive away, because I found a ewe and lamb of his on the lane behind our farm. I have no idea how those sheep got there, and neither did he, but the ewe's lug mark and ear tag told me very clearly it was from Middle Fell. So he came, scratched his head, confessed himself baffled, and took them back.

33

JAMES GREEN.
YEWTREE, WASDALE.

Prefix:—"Yew."

Flock No. 57. Ewes put to the Ram, 250.

A Flock of very old-standing which has always been kept pure. Rams have been used from the Flocks of the late John Richardson, Seathwaite, Borrowdale; Edward Nelson, Gatesgarth; Joseph Richardson, Swinside; John Rothery, Wasdale Head Hall; Thomas Rawling, Lanthwaite Green; William Abbott, Mockerkin; and Teasdale, Hodcarden.

JOHN ROPER.
BOWDERDALE, NETHERWASDALE.

Prefix:—"Box."

Flock No. 58. Ewes put to the Ram, 150.
The usual Flock let with the Farm.

JOHN ROTHERY.
WASDALE HEAD HALL.

Prefix:—"Wastwater."

Flock No. 59. Ewes put to the Ram, 500.

The foundation of this Flock was laid in 1873 by the purchase of Ewes from the late Allan Pearson of Lorton, and these were mated with a Prize-winning Ram named "Samson," bred by and the property of the late John Hodgson of Mockerkin. Sheep were added in 1884 at the dispersal of the last-named Flock. A large number of prize winners have been bred from these Sheep. In 1901 I entered upon the Wasdale Head Hall Farm with the Flock of 754 Sheep which have been held continuously with this Farm for over 300 years.

RICHARD M. WILSON.
MIDDLE ROW, WASDALE HEAD.

Prefix:—"Wasdale."

Flock No. 60. Ewes put to the Ram, 600.

A noted Ram Breeding Flock of old-standing. Many Champion Prize-winners have been bred, including "Old Perfection," "Sampson," and "Double Champion" No. 1900. The last-named was 1st and Champion Herdwick at Bailcliffe Ram Show in 1919, also winning for the best Sheep of any breed, which Class was strongly contested by the Champion of the Blackfaced breed.

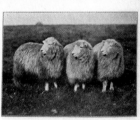

1st PRIZE HERDWICK SHEARLING EWES,
Royal Show at Newcastle, 1908,
the property of The Right Hon. The Earl of Lonsdale.

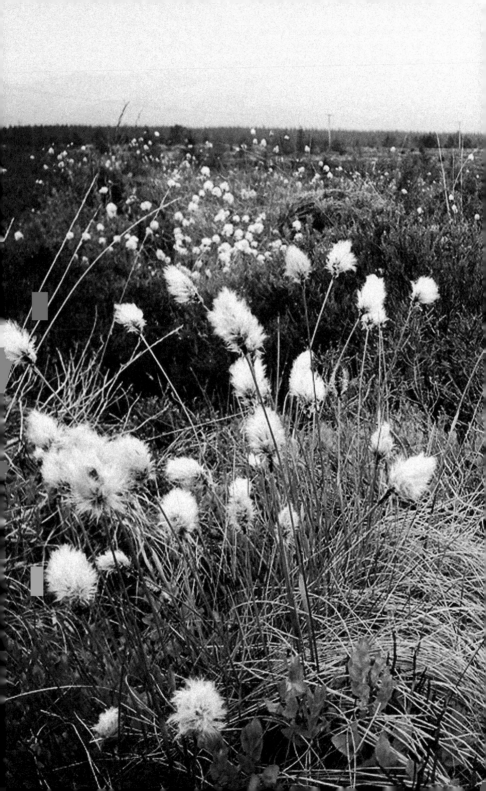

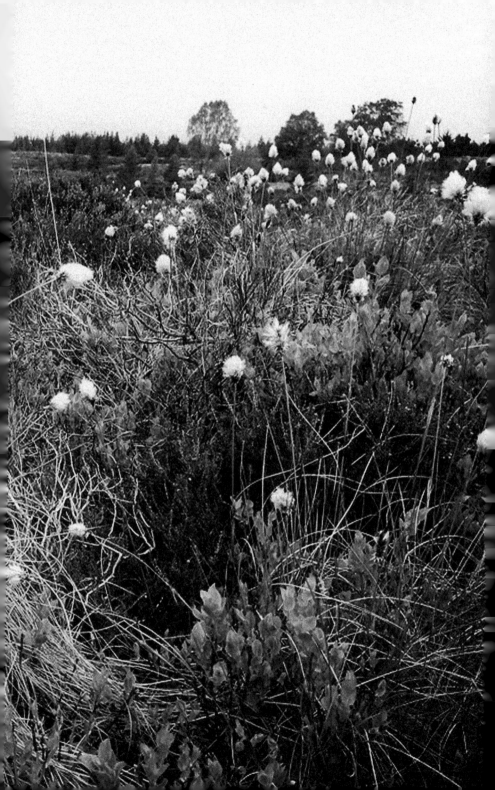

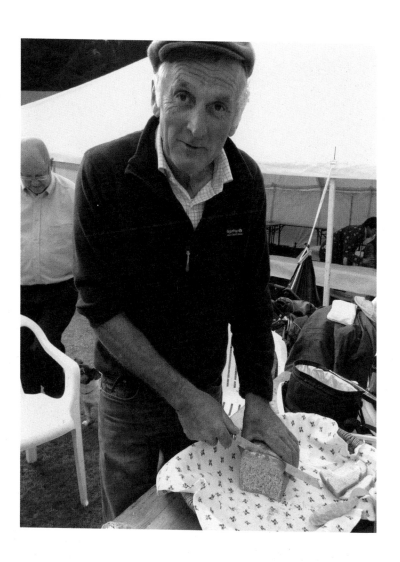

THE SHEPHERDS' BAKING COMPETITION

The shepherding bragging rights in our valley have to be earned at our shepherds' meet, which takes place at the end of August at Patterdale.

I'm all about trying to win the sheep classes. However, a lot of the fun after the sheep show revolves around the "shepherds' baking competition." The shepherds have to bake the prescribed recipe single-handed, without help from the women in their lives.

There is a lively debate each summer at the show organizing committee about what is to be baked. Scotch eggs, says one committee member.

No, says another. Too technical, says a third.

How about rock buns, says a fourth.

No, too easy, says a fifth, scratching his stubble.

Fruit loaf?

Aye.

Yep.

Fine by me.

Everyone sits there with a look of pure concentration, working out who in their families actually bakes fruit loaves, then a twinkle will appear in one or two eyes as they realize that their wife, mother, or grandmother is an expert.

Just as I'm beginning to think the world has gone quite mad and that this can't get any worse, a row breaks out about whether tea breads count as fruit loaves. Half an hour later this remains unresolved, and no one is quite sure whether a tea bread will pass muster with the judge, but as she's apparently been on a TV cooking programme, we think she'll know best.

This year (in remembrance of my dad) we donated a silver cup to the winner of the baking competition, with the inscription "Tom Rebanks Memorial Baking Competition (No Cheating)."

There have been some notorious incidents of cheating, with the baking being done illicitly by grandmothers or next-door neighbours. But in truth, some of the men are fine bakers and take it quite seriously. My dad learned to bake cakes in his final years. He loved trying to win, even if it meant leaving me to make the sheep ready the day before. His proudest baking moment was producing a loaf of beautiful white bread. After the competition he cut it into rough doorknob-thick slices for roast lamb sandwiches off the spit and we ate them to soak up the beer.

Dad passed away last year, but he loved our shepherds' meet, because he had worked with sheep his whole life and all of his shepherding friends came together at it each autumn. I have many happy memories of him in the beer tent after the show. Like me, he had a slightly wicked sense of humour after a couple of drinks, and loved winding people up or creating mischief. Some years he would be sent by my mother to drag me out of the beer tent and take me home before things got out of hand. And like a proper drunk and troublemaker, I would pull him in and we'd stay much longer together.

He is missed.

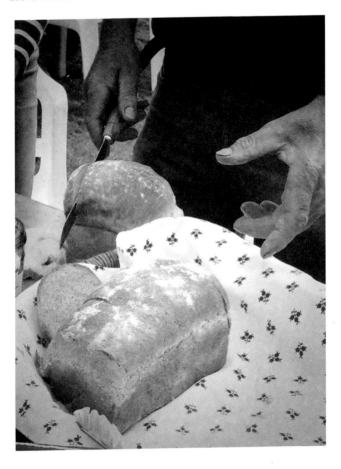

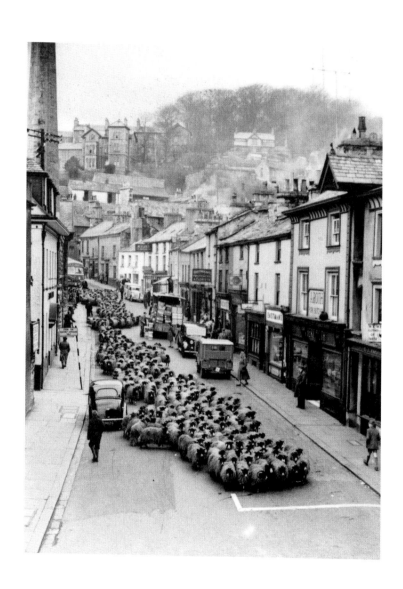

WHY I LOVE THESE
HARDMAN PHOTOS

Until recently most farming families didn't bother much with photographs. Some had a picture of their farm above their mantelpiece, taken from a plane by some enterprising photographer. My grandmother had a tatty old box of family pictures, a few smiling sunburnt faces in the hayfields, or standing proudly at the farmhouse front door, or with a prize sheep or horse. But until recently there was very little pictorial record of what we do.

A few years ago a friend told me about a collection of photos by Joseph Hardman taken between the 1930s and 1960s. He was a freelance photographer for a local newspaper and seems to have been on a quiet mission to capture the local traditions with his camera. He would travel hundreds of miles a week in a taxi, searching for the right light to capture the working life of the Lake District in stylish ways. He photographed shepherds and sheepdogs and shepherds' meets, and work in the hayfields . . . I'm glad he did.

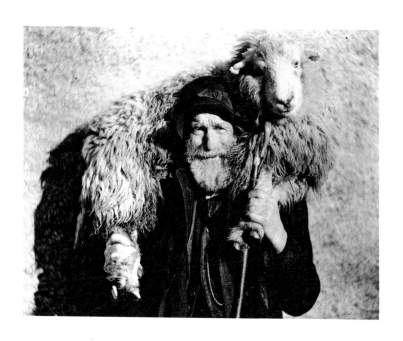

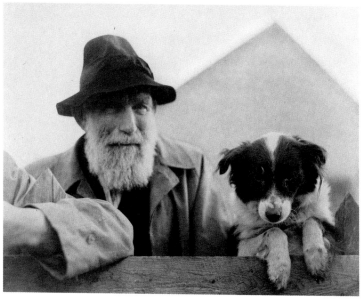

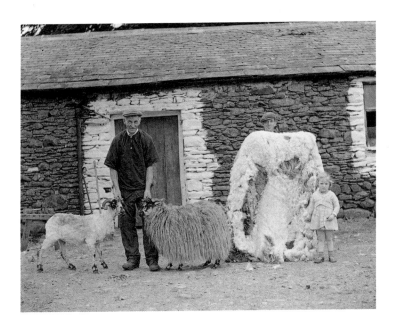

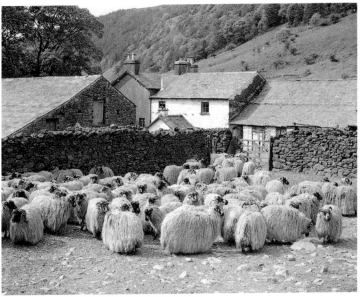

It is tempting to say that these beautiful photos matter because they capture a vanishing world (we are always the "last" shepherds, and have been disappearing for two hundred years in written accounts), but I love them because they capture our living world. I look in the faces of the shepherds in Hardman's pictures and I know I could step into these pictures, join the men, and comment quite easily on the sheep they are discussing.

Last year a lot of farmers came to a party at our house. Helen put these photos on her laptop in a slideshow and left them revolving in the background. Halfway through the evening we noticed that all of the older farmers, and some of the younger ones, too, were circling the laptop, a lively discussion taking place as to where each picture had been taken and who the men and women in each shot were.

My dad liked the clipping day pictures because he had clipped at many of the same places. Each barn, wall, and sheepfold told a story about the families in those places, their past, present, and future.

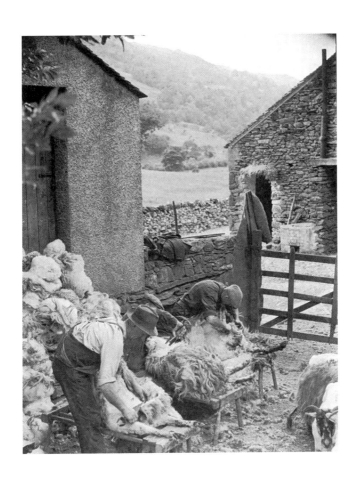

After weeks of grey and brown the valley changes, shape-shifting to something with a dozen shades of green.

The sodden days of winter slip away, and with them the sense of toil and endurance.

The valley is a place of plenty now. The birds sing, and my heart feels that this is my own personal, beautiful spring.

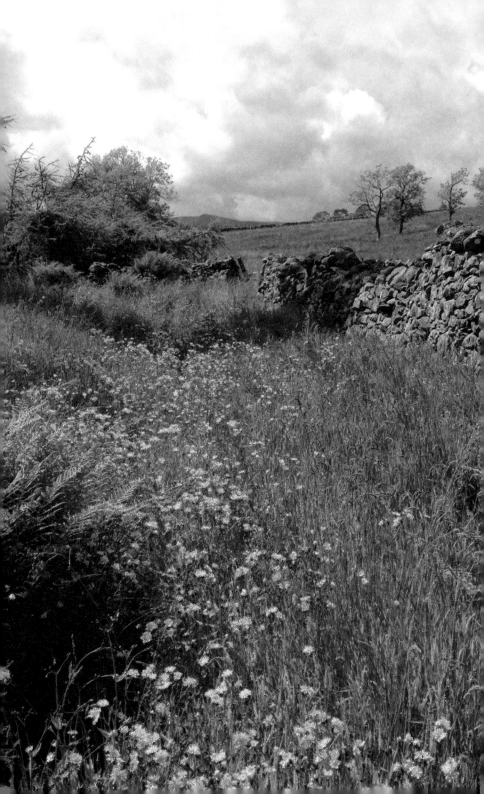

THE PEOPLE

Lake District people are quite distinct from the rest of the English.

To start with we speak differently, with our own dialect that sounds harsher and is full of Norse words. And we are a straightforward lot, with few airs or graces, because we never quite got the same three-tiered class system of much of southern England. It was too poor round here for the aristocrats to oppress us like they did elsewhere. And this freedom has entered our character, because we have a kind of Viking sense of our own worth: we don't doff our caps or show much deference to anyone. I was brought up to avoid Downton Abbey types, not bow to them. A bit like New York taxi drivers, we are famously blunt and straight talking. If I think you are wrong I will tell you.

But mountains also throw people together, because people have to work here as a community, so we are also very sociable. My neighbours always wave when passing, and often stop to talk and swap news. And there are no more decent people to live amongst in the world than my neighbours. When my father died, all of my neighbours, even those I don't always get on with, offered to help in the days after his death, and cakes appeared baked by friends, and when we buried him about four hundred people came from across the north of England. There was a quiet, dignified respect in the air, a reminder that we are bound to each other in a community.

It reminded me that in this half-empty landscape we are surrounded by a plain northern kind of love.

THE BROTHERHOOD
OF THE FELLS

I am alone in the clouds. I have turned around and around until I don't know which way is which. Everything has lost its shape and form, and I know how people get lost and die on mountains. A layer of tiny droplets coats the sheepdogs silver. I send Floss and Tan into the greyness to the left and right of me to ensure we don't let sheep escape. They are wary of heading out of sight, and reappear from time to time with a questioning look.

But surely an army could now march between where I stand and the shepherds to the left and right of me. Then I hear a noise and turn, and half a dozen ewes and lambs tumble past us, fleeing the high ground, presumably cleared by someone else's dogs. I hear a quad bike engine and some whistling, and a silhouette appears against the white backdrop. I breathe and feel safe again.

We make our way down the fell, shoulder to shoulder, two brothers eventually dropping out of the clouds. A threatening grey ceiling hangs above us as we move the flock away home. One by one the other shepherds appear. In front of us is an impressive flock of sheep, somehow gathered despite the weather. Floss comes back and gives me a cuddle, aware that I was nervous and pleased that we can see our work again.

Then we all stop to have our sandwiches, six shepherds on a sodden fell, with wet sheepdogs.

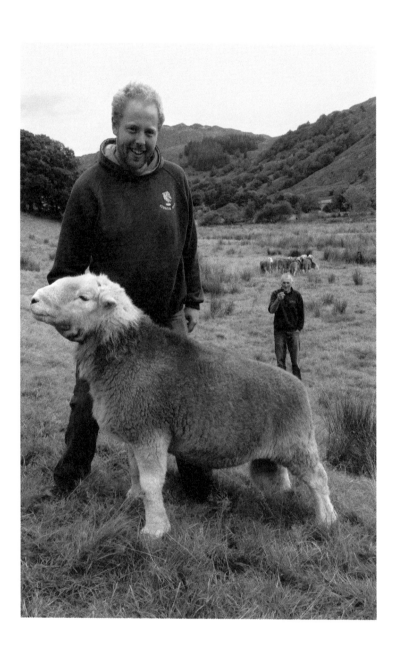

GINGER JOE

One of the rising stars of Lakeland shepherding is Joe Weir. He farms with his father in Borrowdale, at Chapel Farm. When you look at Joe you wouldn't be at all surprised to learn that many of us descend from Vikings. He has a mop of curly ginger hair, often seems to have misplaced his razor, and can be a bit wild when he has had a few beers (can't we all). But he is (and don't tell him I said this) one of the nicest and most honest lads you can meet. He is what we call "keen," meaning that you get the impression he wants to be the top dog in our world. I've told him he might be the second-best shepherd in the Lake District when he grows up, but he tells me to eff off. He already has some great fell dogs, and is sometimes hired to come and gather our fell with us.

Joe has a bad case of tup fever, and from May onwards he starts visiting us about once a week to get a look at our best sheep for the shows and sales. He buys tups from us each autumn, and I wait nervously to hear whether they do well for his flock or not. If they breed good lambs and improve his flock I will be praised, if not, I will be damned. About five years ago

Joe bought one of the best tups of recent times, from the Bland family at West Head. He had to stick his neck out a long way to get it, spending more than five thousand guineas to secure it. He shares it with the noted breeder Willie Richardson at Gatesgarth. That kind of big purchase sends out a statement that you mean business, and that old tup has fathered several show-winning sons and daughters that have gone on to make high prices, more than paying Joe and Willie back. I'm not sure anyone has ever loved an old tup more than Joe loves his.

WILLIE TURBO

Can you learn to be a shepherd?

I'm in the sceptical school on this (sorry, and ignore me if it is your dream). You need a deep understanding of the sheep, place, and people, so sometimes a ten-year-old born to this life is more use than a thirty-year-old graduate of agricultural college who is learning the ropes.

But even those of us who grow up with sheep still have lots to learn, so we support an apprenticeship scheme for young shepherds.

Two days a week we get sent a scruffy, short-legged, and overly talkative twenty-year-old called William Tyson.

The Tysons are Herdwick royalty. William's ancestor Derwent Tyson won over three thousand rosettes at shows with his sheep. Respect where respect is due.

But when William started working for us, he had a reputation for being sort of stuck in bottom gear. "Steady, very steady" was how he was described to us. A neighbour watching him working with our sheep sarcastically christened him "Willie Turbo."

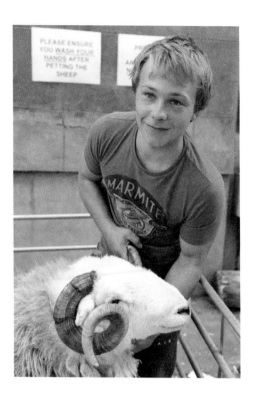

As you may have already guessed, being an apprentice is a bottom-rung-of-the-ladder type of experience, with many reminders that you have a lot to learn. I'm hardly out of shepherding basic class and I'm keeping his feet on the ground until he knows enough to be treated with a bit more respect. Anyway, we tease him a lot.

William usually brings his own packed lunch. Often it consists of two packets of crisps and a chocolate biscuit. He empties the different-flavoured packets of crisps into his bait tub and calls it a "crisp salad."

He might not be the fastest, but he is conscientious, care-

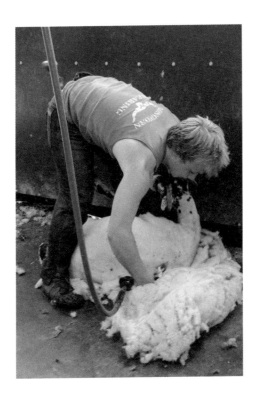

ful, and observant when working with the sheep, and those are valuable attributes. He's becoming a good shepherd. The young men and women doing the apprenticeship scheme are the future of our way of life, so when I am not giving him hell, encouraging him to work faster, and pointing out things he could do better, I try and teach him the things I know that the older shepherds taught me. We are all only as good as the things we know, or as good as the last day's work we did.

Sometimes Willie Turbo teaches me things that he has learnt on other farms. I'm thinking of rechristening him "Willie Half-Speed," to reflect his considerable progress.

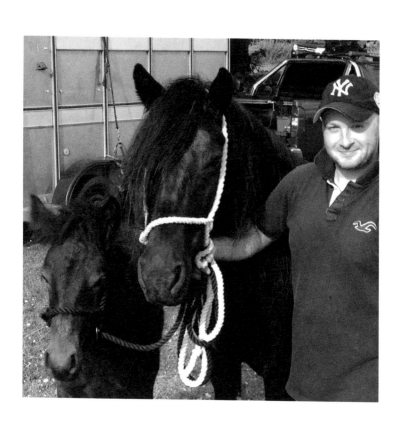

ROBERT AND HIS FELL PONIES

He doesn't reckon much of sheep, my friend Robert. He thinks they eat his horse pasture and winter hay. Instead, he lives and breathes fell ponies, the native ponies of the Lakeland fells. He is as obsessed with them as I am with sheep. He works nights in a dessert factory a few miles away and crosses paths with me each morning—me heading round my flock, him tending to his ponies before going home for some rest. These amazing, tough animals were once the workhorses of the area. They were ridden everywhere and carried wool over the fells in caravans to the towns where it was processed. They pulled ploughs and carts, and led in the hay for winter, and they, like our Herdwick sheep, had to do all of that and live on iron rations out on the fells, fending for themselves. A few dozen enthusiasts like Robert have kept these special ponies going, decades after tractors replaced them on the farms. Robert is the fourth generation of his family to breed, show, and sell fell ponies under the "Birkett Bank" herd prefix. When I tell him he should sell them, get a grip, and buy some Herdwicks, he tells me to bugger off.

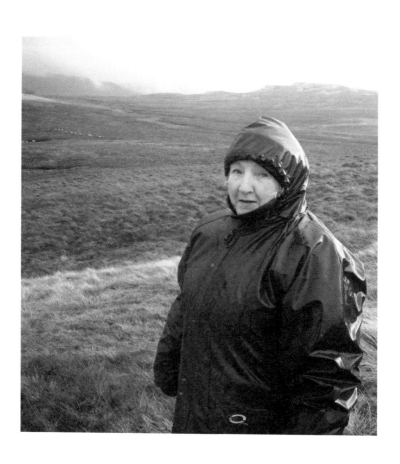

JEAN WILSON:
QUEEN OF HERDWICKS

Jean Wilson is a shoot-first-and-ask-questions-afterwards kind of a lady. If she thinks you are doing something wrong, she will happily tell you are "bloody useless." She calls me "James Rebanks," as if I am a naughty schoolboy she needs to keep an eye on. Some folk are slightly scared of her, but I have long since learnt that if you earn her respect and stand your ground, she is a pussycat.

It usually starts with her silver-grey pickup truck coming down the road. She will spot us working in the sheep pens or a field. Then she stops and shouts, "What's going on today, then?" There isn't much that happens in our corner of the Lake District that Jean doesn't know about. It's the bush telegraph, gossip and news travelling by word of mouth between farm trucks as we go about our work.

Jean is one of a long line of tough northern shepherding women who can go toe-to-toe with the men and often beat them. She is such a big character that until about a decade ago we still called her "Jean Maxwell," her maiden name somehow sticking despite decades of marriage. She is fiercely proud of, and competitive with, her flock of Herdwick sheep.

There is a fairly spicy rivalry between us. To earn her respect you have to try and beat her, but don't expect her to make it easy, or to like it when it happens. When I first beat her with Herdwick sheep at our local show in 2006, I knew I had landed a significant blow because she would barely speak to me for a month. Last year I won our shepherds' meet and when she next came for a cup of coffee, I arranged for the silver cup to be on the table next to where she sits, to remind her. She nearly choked on her biscuit. A few minutes later, she handed me a piece of chocolate tiffin she had brought with her, and as I ate she smirked, and I realized it had been given to me on a silver tray she had won at Keswick Show. "You haven't ever won that," she gloated.

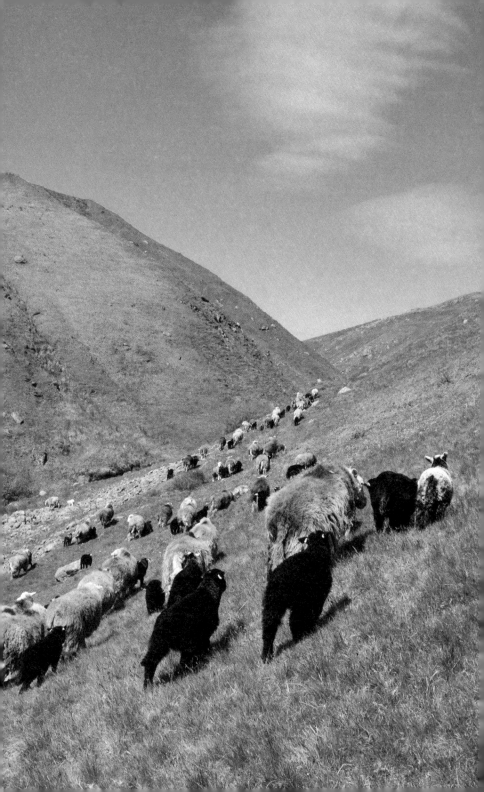

"SUNSHINE"

One of our best friends is called Derek Wilson, but to many of us he is "Sunshine." His wife is Jean Wilson, Queen of the Herdwicks, but he says he has had enough of sheep work. After decades of being press-ganged into washing and preening sheep for shows, he is now in full-scale revolt, and refuses to take part in the sheep proceedings. Instead, he does what he likes to do, which is to be everyone's favourite farming handyman and fixer. He loves mending and building things. There will be hardly a field in this valley that Derek hasn't worked in, hardly a gate he hasn't hung, and hardly a wall he hasn't rebuilt from time to time. I recently caught him with his tractor stuck at an awful angle in a stream, with him trying to drive it out on a giant piece of lumber he had dragged there to help.

"What the hell you doing?" I bawled. "You'll kill yourself!"

"I'm doing all right, just hold that sleeper and stop blathering," he replied.

He was repairing a water gate over the stream and thought this all entirely normal behaviour.

Derek must be about ninety years old, though he works like

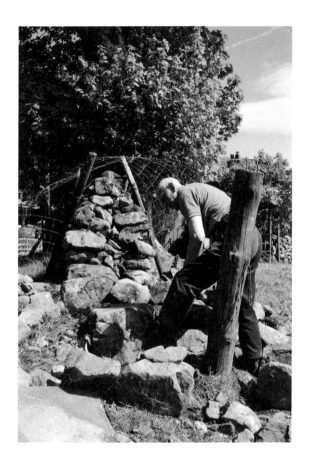

an eighteen-year-old. He and my dad used to work together quite a bit, and had various scrapes, including the time my dad almost killed him with a hammer when Derek got his head in the way of the nail. Some time ago, the Wilson sisters, who farm over the hill from us, played a trick on him and sent a phoney letter asking him, on behalf of the authorities, if he were available to "rebuild Hadrian's Wall," because there weren't many people with the "appropriate walling skills." Although he now denies it, we think he swallowed it hook, line, and sinker.

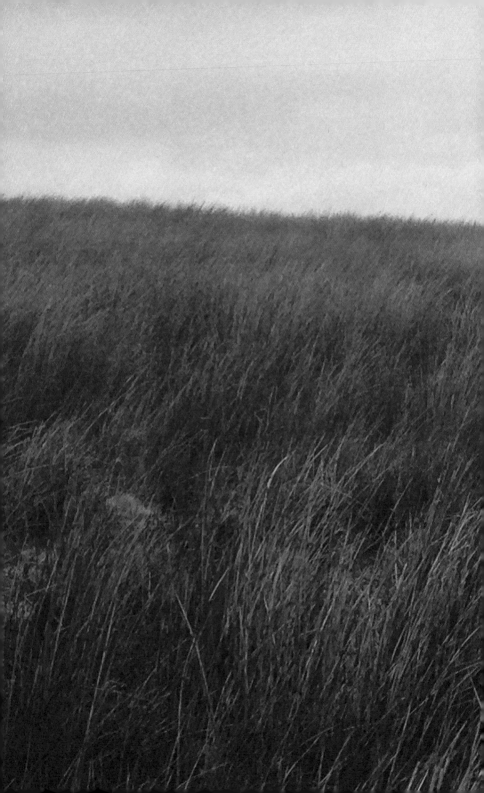

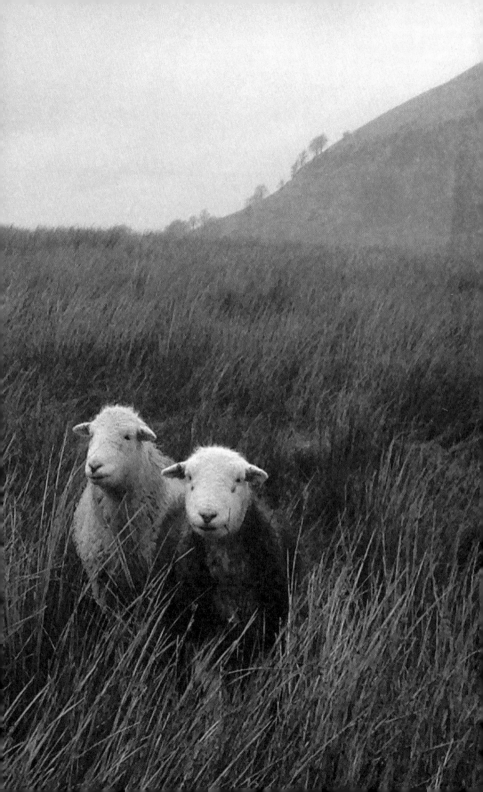

The ewes and lambs tumble down the rocky screes,
lost from sight in the bracken, a waist-high
ocean of green.

They pass on down, a shadowed parting of ferns
and fronds.

I see them again, down below in the open ground,
on the short-cropped grass, as they race away
to the rest of the flock, a river of white and
grey flowing home.

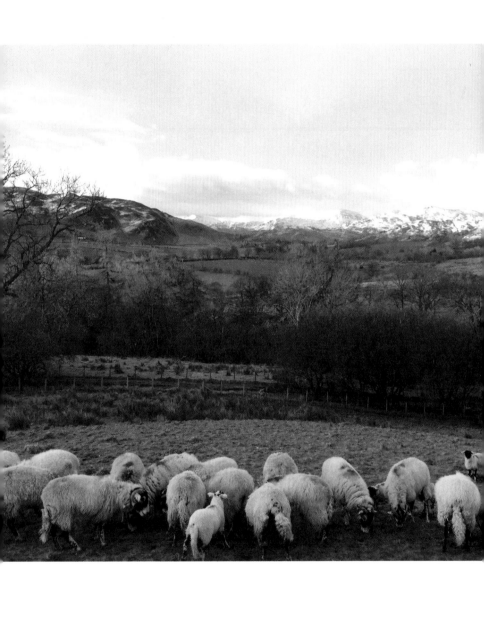

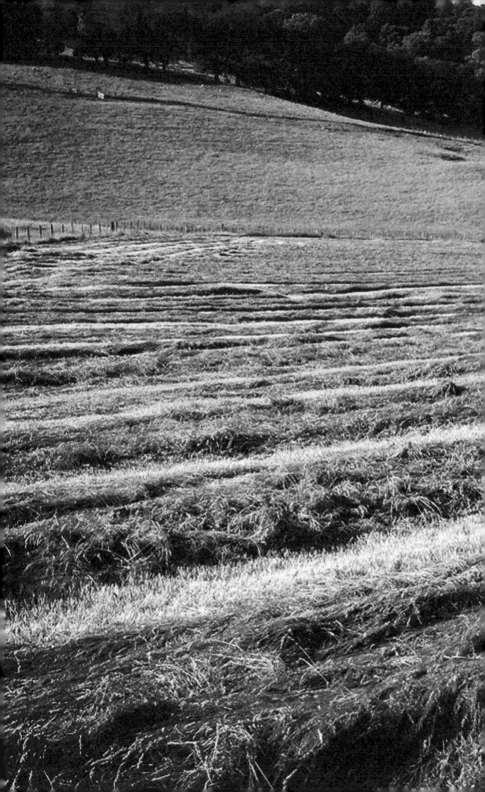

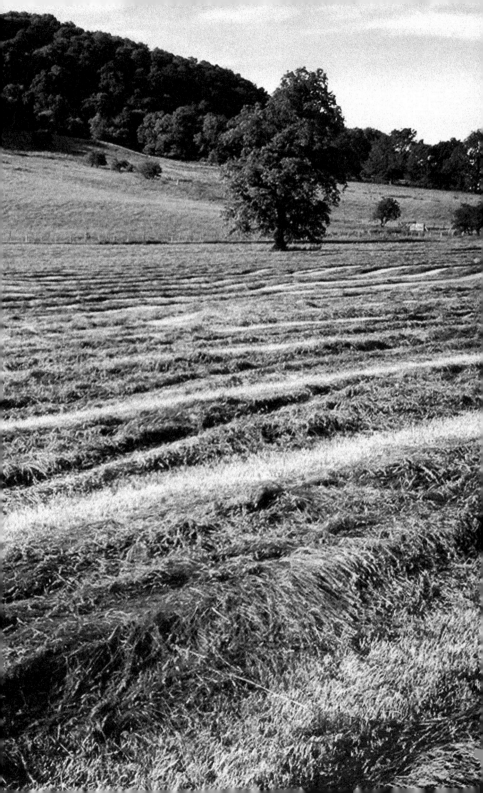

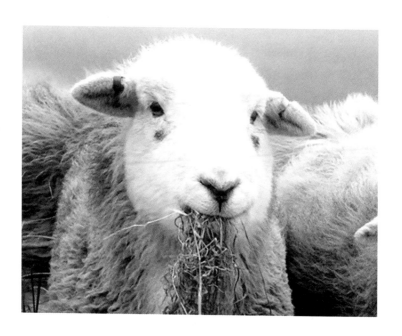

SHEPHERD'S PIE

Truth be told, I don't like shepherd's pie. I know this is a bit like Kim Kardashian saying she doesn't like shopping, but it's true. In fact, I'm not that keen on any of the old-fashioned English stews made with lamb. I grew up in a traditional farming family in which money was tight, and before "foreign" food and fancy cooking had taken hold in the British diet. So we ate our own lamb—a lot. And there was a limited range of dishes, too: greyish stews or mince in gravy, and mashed potato with everything. I was a picky eater, but was made to eat it. I protested by chewing the stew or mince endlessly until it was like a kind of cardboard and my jaw hurt. Then I would be told off and sent to the back kitchen, where I would spit it out for the dog and pretend I had eaten it.

My mother howls in outrage when I say we ate stew all the time, and says it isn't true, but anyway that's how I remember it. And my absolute hell was shepherd's pie (minced lamb or beef, covered in an inch of mashed potato and cooked in the oven until it has skin baked on the top). Then, when I was about twenty years old, there was a kind of quiet revolution in how we ate, and suddenly the same lamb that I had grown to hate was turned into other tasty dishes, like curries, tagines, and lasagnes. The elders in my family were very suspicious of this change, but I loved it. It made me fall in love with the food we produce again. Some change is good.

I'm really hoping that someone starts to air-dry Herdwick hams again. They did it in the chimney in the old days, making something that tasted a little like Parma ham. Today we regularly eat our own Herdwick lamb: it is delicious, but best slow-cooked and always treated with respect. And Helen is converting me to tasty stews (she calls them tagines) and insists I'm wrong about all of this stuff.

My mother remains annoyed.

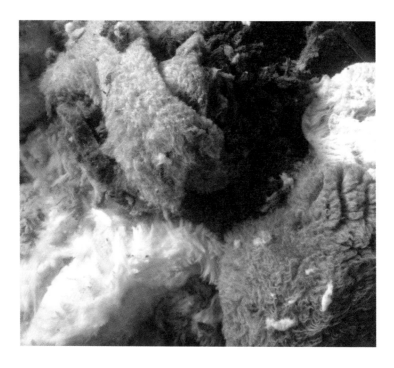

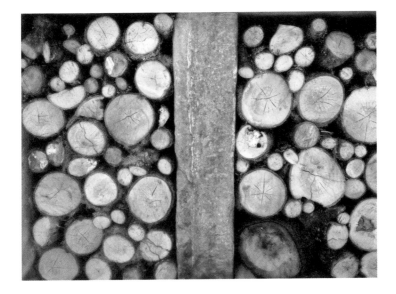

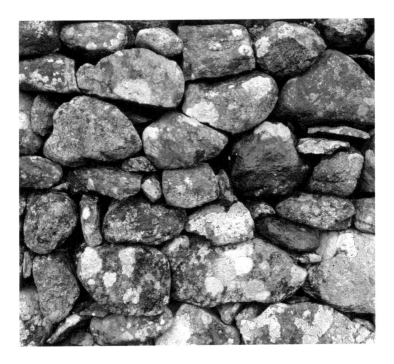

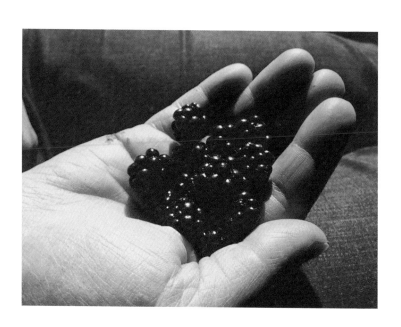

PICKING BRAMBLES

England has the best puddings in the world, but the best of all is apple and bramble crumble with custard. It should be made the old-fashioned way, with the topping made out of flour, butter, and sugar in a thick biscuitlike layer. There should be no messing about with almonds, oats, cinnamon, and other semi-poisonous trash. The crumble tastes best if you pick your own brambles (you may call them blackberries—I'm not sure why) from the dykes, and steal the apples from a neighbour's apple tree. We usually have an expedition to pick the brambles in September or October. The bushes they grow on line the lanes here and have thick tangles of thorns that grab your clothes and scratch your skin. My kids stuff their mouths with them and end up with fingers stained purple.

Seamus Heaney once wrote a poem in which he said that summer's blood was in the brambles he picked as a child, which is one of those lines that, once heard, is never forgotten.

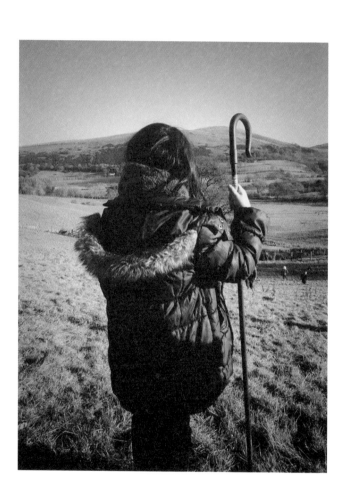

THE FREEDOM OF BIRDS

Two years ago we began to open our farm up for school and nursery visits. We are aware how lucky we are to live in such a beautiful place and we thought we'd share a little of the life we live. We started to work with about ten schools to give kids a taste of what farming is about.

We built a classroom space in the barn, along with the necessary toilets—"tups" for boys and "yows" for girls. We spent many hours thinking about what the kids should learn. We read the National Curriculum and interviewed teachers, and earnestly tried to develop a set of themes and activities that were sufficiently worthy. With hindsight, we went a bit Jamie Oliver . . .

We wanted to explain how farming works, where food and other products like wool come from, how the land is managed, the changing farming year, and the "cultural significance" of the Lake District. We developed outdoor sessions where the kids can find and learn about the creatures that live in the woods, becks, and meadows.

We show them the work we do with the sheep and explain

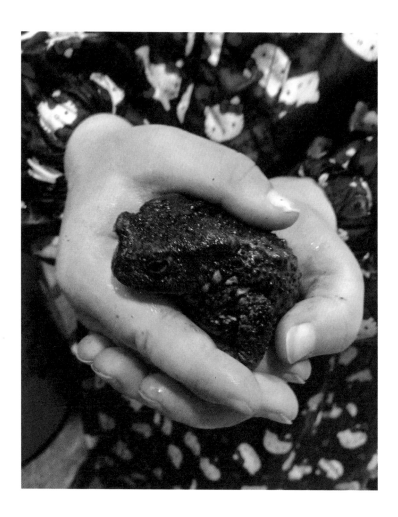

how the landscape works. They do simple things like collect the chicken eggs, feed the pet lambs, make things from wool, draw animals, or go on treasure hunts to find interesting objects. As a lazy afterthought, we decided that at lunchtime they could run free in the field beneath our farmyard.

At school the next day, when the children are asked by their teachers what they enjoyed the most, the same answer comes back time and again: what the children love the most is running free for forty-five minutes in a field. And after all our hand-wringing about what they should "learn."

I like to watch them running around, tumbling and getting dirty hands or wet knees. Sometimes they spread their arms out, like wings, and run down the hill as if they are flying. One little boy came running back to his teacher, red-faced, and shouted, "Look, Miss! We're like birds!" The teacher turned to me and said, "You know, hardly any of them have ever been this free before. It's amazing."

When I hear this, I am not sure whether to laugh with joy or to cry with despair, because something so simple, so normal to previous generations, is now vanishingly rare for so many children. What kind of world have we created? Everyone should have a place where they can spread their wings and fly.

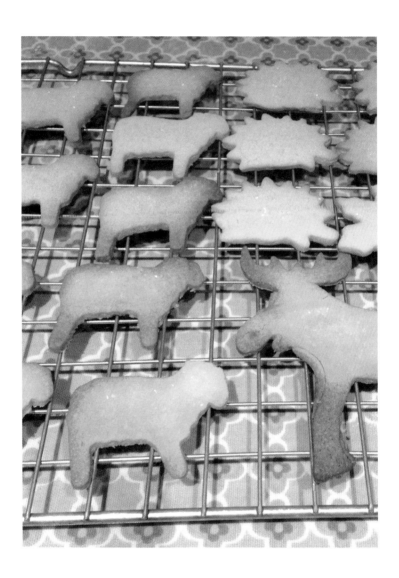

MAKING PEG SHEEP, MASKS, AND BISCUITS

When school groups come to the farm, we get them to make their own mini-flock of sheep out of washing line pegs, cardboard, glue, and wool. What could possibly go wrong with thirty kids, a sheep's fleece, and a glue gun?

Initially the kids look a bit scared of wool. They touch it like it might be radioactive or really smelly, but after ten minutes they are tugging it and pulling it into little strands, weaving it with their fingers, curling it around cardboard, gluing and pegging it into shape. They use a glue gun to stick the paper hand-drawn heads onto the woollen bodies (or to stick each other to things).

The sheep they make are quite funny, with wonky legs, funky colours, and huge grinning faces. Sometimes the sheep have multiple eyes or stick their tongues out cheekily, and once a kid made a sheep that looked suspiciously like Hitler. When they go home, they take their funny sheep with them as a keepsake from the farm. Sometimes we get the kids to make sheep biscuits, which is even more messy. And each year one school comes to make sheep masks for a festival in our local town, when they march through the darkness disguised as sheep, with the route lit by torches and lanterns.

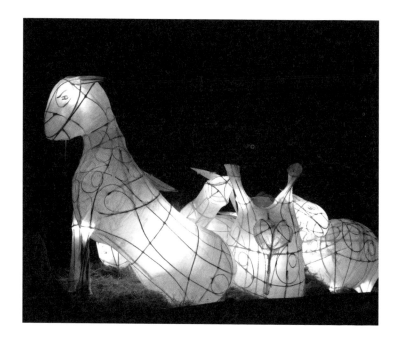

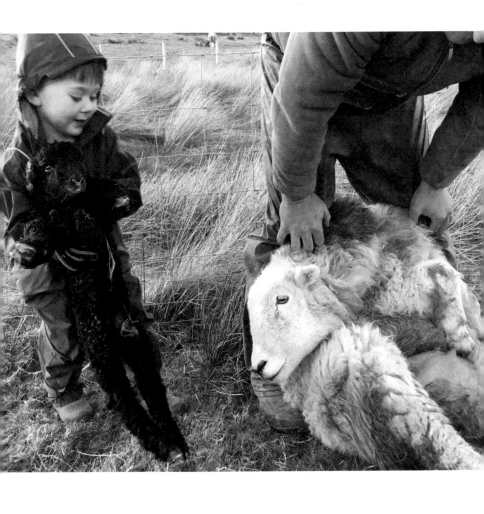

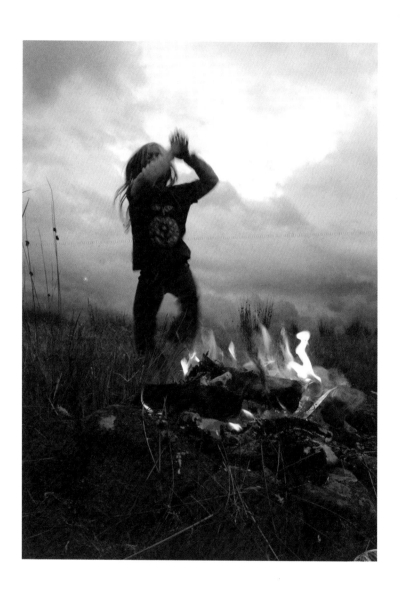

WILD KIDS

It is quite hard to get away on holiday if you have a farm; sometimes you just don't have time for a break. So last summer we decided to buy a tent and have a "camping trip" at home. We put the tent up in a hidden place across the fields and built a campfire. The kids went wild roaming around the field and informed us that they were "Indians." As it got dark, they danced around the glowing fire like little pagans. Then, when they were worn out, we all went to bed to the sound of the ewes calling the lambs across the fields. It rained all night, and I woke at 4 a.m. to drops of rain thudding on the groundsheet from a puddle that had formed in the roof of my badly erected tent. The kids woke up, damp and cold, and started scratching their midge bites. They demanded to go home, and when we got there we realized that Helen had given up hours earlier and was tucked up warmly in bed. The kids don't remember it quite how I do—they love "camping" and want to go again this summer.

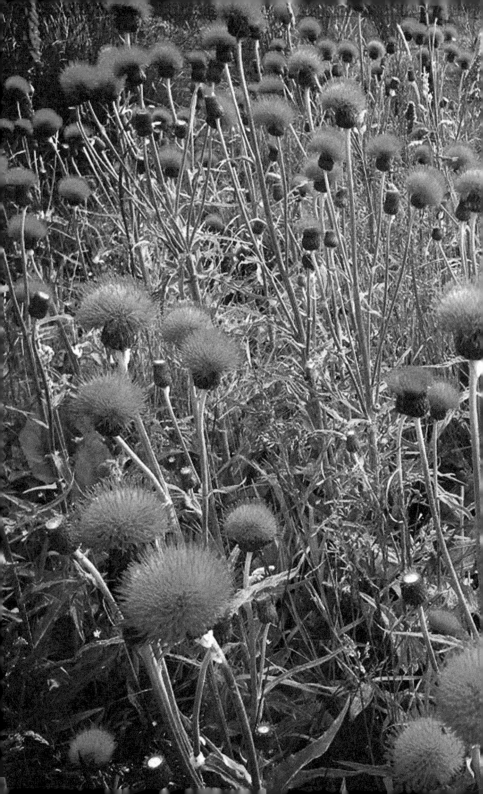

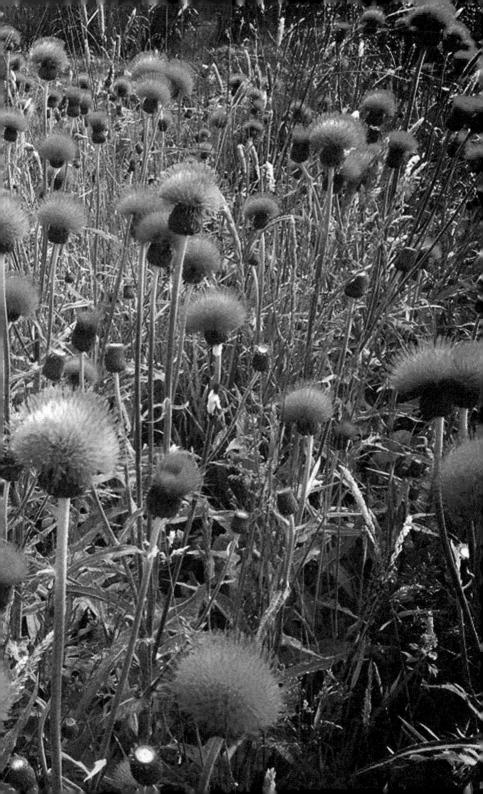

The hay is baled and stacked in the barn and the empty fields stand quiet. Tractors have been returned to the yard and men and women have gone back to their homes.

The life of the meadow has withdrawn to the field verges and the banks of the beck, which trickles halfheartedly away to the sea, each remaining pool alive with minnows.

There is a sense of relief in my stomach now the winter crop is made and safe from the rain. So I don't mind at all when fat drops flop down and kick up dust by my feet.

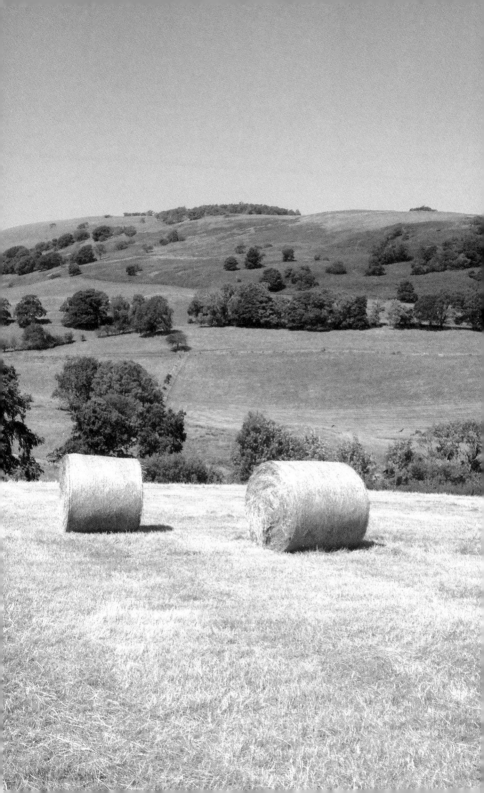

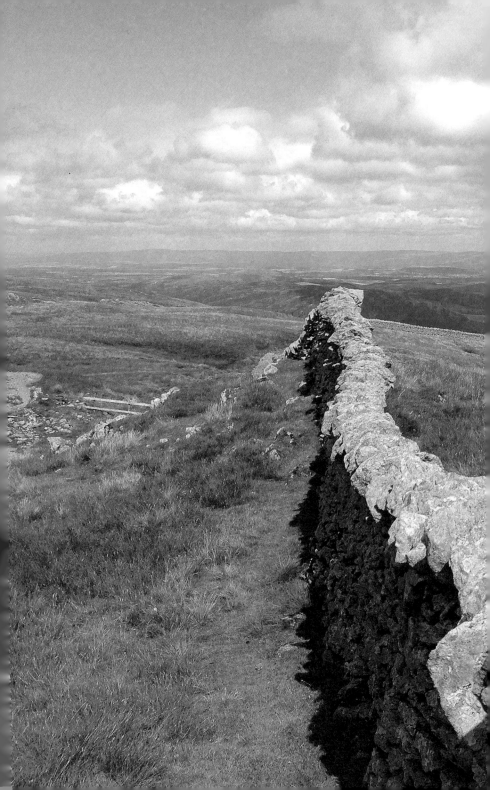

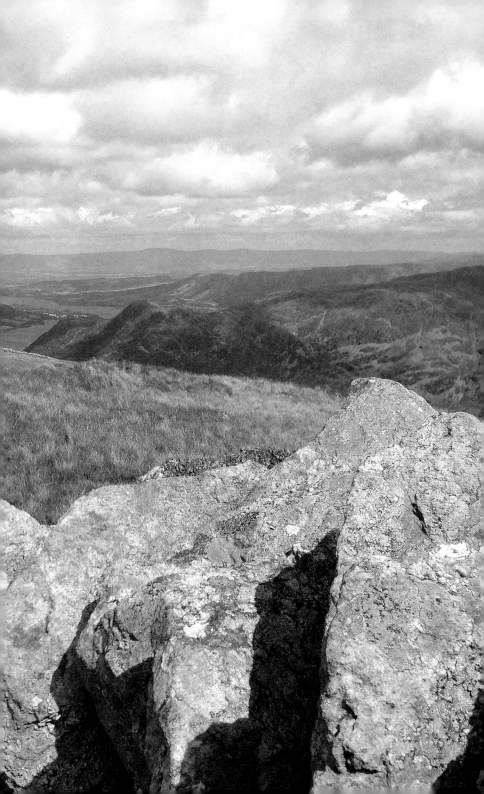

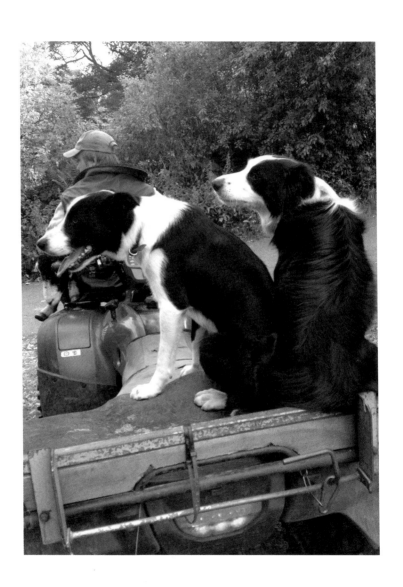

WHAT ARE SHEEPDOGS
FOR EXACTLY?

You simply can't be a proper shepherd without a sheepdog.

They are an indispensable part of a shepherd's life. Several times a day I need to catch a sheep, or move some sheep from one field to another. If you've ever tried to move half-wild mountain sheep without a dog you will know that a man can't run as fast as a sheep, and they will simply cease to move as a flock and will break away in all directions until you are left cussing and yelling, and jumping up and down like a maniac. On the fells where we farm, two hundred people couldn't gather the sheep from the crags, cliffs, and moorland that they range across.

The sheepdogs are an extension of the shepherd's mind and arms. They can climb up the crags and work semi-independently of the shepherd. They can make their own judgements about going back further in any direction if they see sheep the shepherd can't. They can work in torrential rain, snow, wind, or any other conditions. They can "hunt" across ground covered in scrub or bracken and find sheep. They can run much faster than man or sheep, and for much longer.

And crucially, they instil in the sheep the flocking instinct because wolves and sheep evolved together, so the sheep behave themselves and gather into a flock that is manageable and controlled. All that is good about a sheepdog is based on the instincts of a wolf, their wild ancestor, channelled and controlled through selective breeding, training, and discipline into something productive and useful. They are the ultimate low-tech solution, and they do it all for a little praise, an occasional pat, and a bowl of dog food.

And were I to be caught in a snowstorm and need to dig in, I can send Floss home for help, or huddle with the dogs and keep warm under the snow to stay alive. I have even heard of sheepdogs putting themselves between an angry cow or bull and their master, to protect them from being charged.

Little wonder that we shepherds often love our sheepdogs like they are our best friends.

MY DOGS

FLOSS

Floss is a tough cookie. When she was six months old she had a terrible accident, falling off the back of the ATV quad bike and twisting her leg horribly, breaking it in several places. We rushed her to the vets, and they operated on her, putting in pins and metalwork. They didn't know if they could save the leg, but they tried. I was brokenhearted. In the days to come I went every day to the vets to see her and hear about her progress, and she would wag her tail and smile at me. Everyone in the veterinary centre fell in love with her because she is so pretty and kind natured. After a few days it became apparent that she might lose some of the feeling in her lower leg because the break had perhaps severed some vital veins. I gave her a cuddle, and she sighed deeply like she knew.

We brought her home unsure what would happen when the plaster came off. She lay by the fire, pleased to be home, getting lots of love, but desperately sad each morning when I went to the flock without her. After a few weeks the plaster cast came

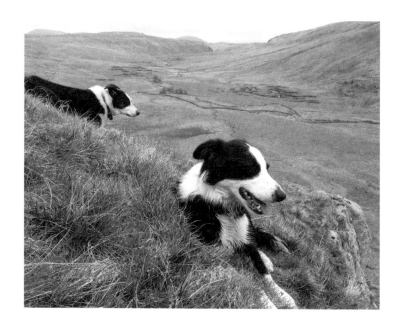

off, and her withered leg hung limply, unused and seemingly hopeless. But we did what the vets told us, and massaged it and washed it every day. Slowly she began to use it, and it began to resemble a leg more each day. After another week or two her leg looked much healthier, and she was using it. And I could no longer stop her coming with me to the farm, as she lives to work. She still has a slight limp when she walks on hard surfaces, but she has a full working life, and you would never know she'd been wounded if you saw her work in the fields.

She is a field dog, amazingly confident in the valley bottom fields where she knows the boundaries and the sheep are always in sight of her powerful eye. But she doesn't think working on vast unfenced fells and moors befits her talents, and she goes sulky. I forgive her this, because, as the old shepherds say, there isn't a dog or a man born without a fault.

I think I see the sheep groan when she comes to work. They know that she is very good, and they have to do what they are told. Floss is a strong character. Wilful. She is absolutely convinced that however many other dogs are in attendance, she is the top dog and they should respect her authority. She is a wonderful sheepdog, and I suspect I may look back on her when I am old and know that she was a once-in-a-lifetime dog.

TAN

Tan is a completely different character to Floss. He is a gentle, almost timid dog. His coat is smooth and shorter than Floss's. He is an athletic dog, with a lot of strength. He can jump a five-bar gate or a fence easily. If you looked at Floss and Tan together you'd think Tan would be the Alpha, the top dog, but that isn't so. Floss is the boss, and Tan shows a gentlemanly respect for her authority. If Floss is working, Tan will hold back behind her and let her take the lead. He will even slow down to respect that she is slower. So he does his best work when I take him separately from Floss.

Once the boss is out of the way, he becomes a great working dog, obedient, hardworking, and fast. Unlike Floss, who thinks she knows best nearly all of the time, Tan will do exactly what I tell him always. If I send him backwards over a fell (mountain) he will keep going back until long out of sight. A couple of times I have lost him and then half an hour later he has reappeared with a small flock of sheep that he has found way back in the rocks.

Floss and Tan ride with me on my ATV quad bike almost everywhere. This saves their legs for when it matters, and we can as a team cover a lot more ground than shepherds in the old days when they would have been on foot or on a fell pony. Last summer, a shepherd friend came to see my show sheep in a large field. We parked by the road, and I sent Tan round the sheep. He jumped the fence and bolted away round the boundary like Usain Bolt. The sheep were wild and tried to escape through a hedge, but he jumped that and brought the strays back, and then the small flock down the rough ground to where we were standing. I hadn't thought much of this, because I see it all the time, but my friend was clearly impressed. He gave the sheep a quick polite look, and then began trying to buy Tan.

"No chance," I told him. "They haven't made enough money yet to make me sell him."

I once tried to buy a great sheep from an old shepherd.

I offered him a ridiculous price for it, figuring that it would help me establish my young flock, and its descendants might pay me back in the long term. Anything less than a high price and he would not be interested.

After my bid he smiled at me with some pity, and then said gently, "But what would I do with the money that would be better than owning that sheep?"

And then I realised that he had no interest in money at all.

I've heard it said that everything has a price. But when it comes to great sheep and sheepdogs, money isn't enough.

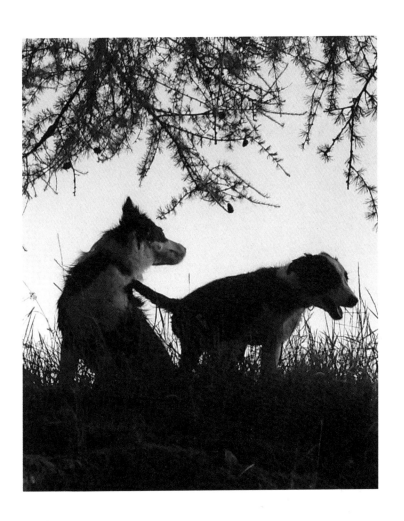

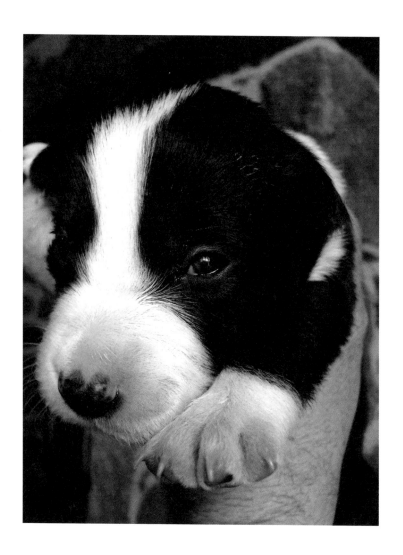

PUPPIES

A lot of joy in farming is about the new stories always starting. The flock, farmers, and sheepdogs renew themselves in an
ever-revolving cycle of birth, life, and death. A good sheepdog might live ten years, so a shepherd will only work with
a handful in a lifetime and each one becomes a dear friend.
When they die, we lose a member of the family.

So I always planned to have puppies from Floss, because I
wanted to ensure that she was the first of a dynasty of sheepdogs that could work with me for many years to come. Floss
is hardwired to herd sheep. She couldn't help herself even as
a pup, and her puppies are the same. She had ten of them,
which began arriving while we were having our supper. She
licked and cleaned them endlessly, suffered their grabbing of
her nipples, and was patient with their endless attempts to get
squashed under her body. But by the time they were a month
old she was ready for a break, and would look pleadingly at me
when I left the farmhouse each morning. "Oh, go on then, old
girl," I'd say, and she would come with me.

I have kept two of those pups: one that looks like their father, Tan, and one that is the double of Floss. The other eight have gone to new homes now, to other respected shepherds or people we trust to give them active, stimulating lives in the outdoors.

I named my two pups Meg and Skye. Each day I take them for two long walks, teaching them to come back to me when called, to have some control before we go near any sheep. At least, that is what I am meant to be doing. But they have the same instincts as their parents, and if they set eyes on a sheep, even a couple of fields away, their tails drop, they crouch forwards, and they start drawing closer. Last night a stray sheep met us on the lane. The two pups couldn't help themselves and bolted off after it, its movement an irresistible force to be followed. They brought it back a few moments later, not entirely sure what they had done, or why, but very pleased with themselves. Floss seemed to smile, saying they're going to be okay.

In the weeks to come, my job is to teach them carefully the things they need to know without exposing them to any knocks or scares that could destroy their confidence. Some people don't start training their dogs until they are nearly a year old, but Floss was half trained at six months old. I would love to take credit, but in truth the instinct is deep inside her.

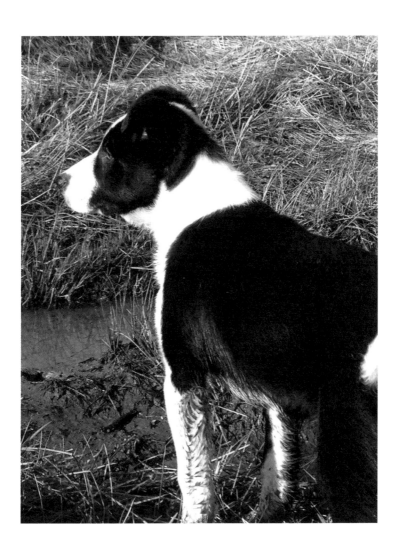

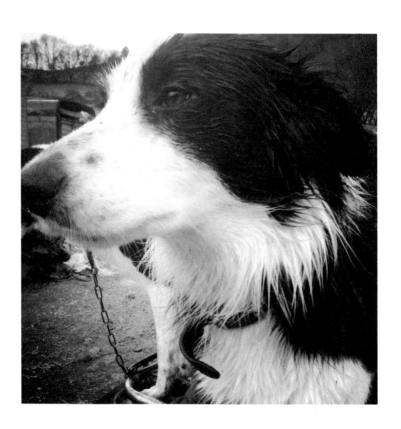

HOW TO SPEAK SHEEPDOG

If you see sheepdogs working on TV it tends to be a rather civilized and elegant business, but that isn't how it always looks in real life. My dad once had a sheepdog with the nickname "Mac the Bastard," because a friend once heard him bawling at it across a hillside: "Mac, come here, you bastard."

One of my neighbours calls his sheepdog "Dog." His commands consist of "Dog," said in different tones, with a range of wild gesticulations with his hands. I am old-fashioned and like to use more conventional commands:

Come here: Please come to me right now. (It is not good if the dog keeps going over the horizon.)

Lie down: Please stop and drop to the ground, because you have gone crazy, the sheep are scattering, and if you don't lie down right now they will be halfway to Manchester. "Lie down," said again, means "If you don't stop right now you're sacked."

Stay: Please freeze right now, and don't move a muscle. I once heard an old shepherd say his dog was so obedient that he forgot he had told it to stay by some sheep—until he came back the next day and it was still holding them in the same place.

Away: Please go in a counterclockwise direction around the sheep (God only knows how sheepdogs know what counterclockwise is).

Come by: Please go in a clockwise direction around the sheep (opposite of the above). Do not jump over the fence at the far end and keep going into the sunset. My grandfather's dog Tosh sometimes didn't come back and would have to be retrieved a day or two later from the village, where he had gone to mate with a bitch in heat.

Go bye: I don't use this. My dad used to drive me mad by using "go bye" for both directions (instead of "come by" and "away"), and my dogs used to look at him as if he were an idiot. I'd teach my dad the right commands and then five minutes later he would be saying "go bye" again, proving that you might be able to teach old dogs new tricks, but not an old shepherd.

Look back: I can see sheep that you can't. You didn't go far enough, so turn around, you idiot, and look back to where they are. Sometimes the dog looks back as if to say, I'm the one up here, mate, and I'm telling you this is the best we are going to do.

Steady: Slow down, or the sheep will jump the wall into the vicarage or the back gardens of incomers and I will be getting angry phone calls and threats of insurance claims all evening.

Heel: I don't want you to do anything just yet, so walk at my heels, almost touching my leg, and stay there, because I don't want you running about upsetting sheep.

Bike: I know you can't drive it, but get on the quad bike and stay there.

Bed: Go straight to your kennel. You are an idiot, doing more harm than good. Stay in your kennel. Never come out of your kennel again.

Good dog, you did all right: Oh my God, you are amazing. I've never seen better sheepdog work. If I had to choose right now between my wife and you, she's packing her bags and you can come in to watch TV.

NB: A good dog hangs on your every word. A great dog sometimes knows best and does what needs doing, no matter what you've said. We call this a "clever fucker," but if it ignores you and is wrong, a "useless fucker."

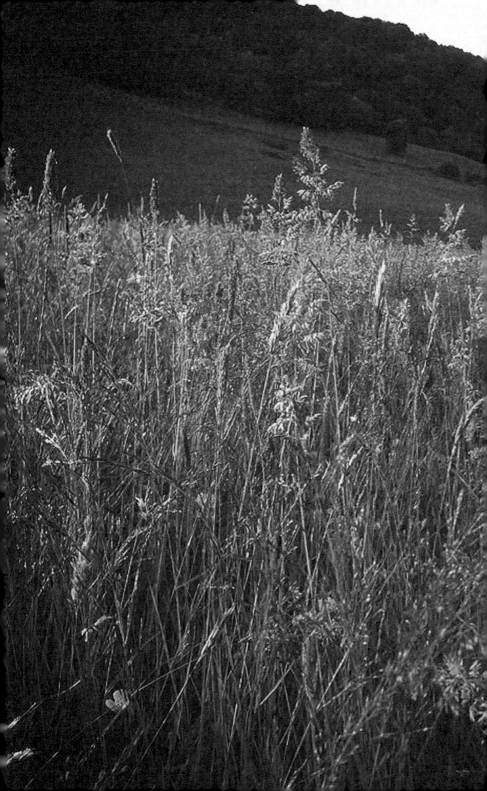

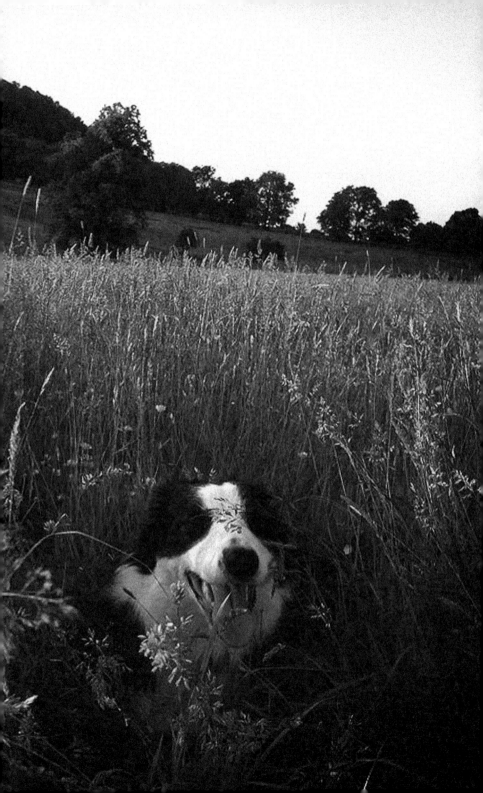

NESTS

One of the nicest things about working outside for long hours is getting to know the wildlife that lives in the fields and farmyard. I've built up a mental map of where I see the robin each day, or which window the swallows dart out from in the barns, or which crack in the house wall a blue tit emerges from. I see the oystercatcher perched on the top of a gate stoop keeping its eggs warm and the skylark flitting upwards from a tuft of grass. My grandfather used to love pointing out these everyday miracles.

This summer I have been keeping an eye on three nests: a chaffinch that has nested in some hurdles by my barn, a swallow that has nested in the eaves of my new sheep shed, and a pied wagtail that has nested behind some logs by my bedroom window. But the best of all is a pair of barn owls in a tree nest box we put there specially for them. It is a joy to see the barn owls return. It suggests to me that our new conservation woodland areas and hedgerows have helped.

Being surrounded by wild things is a part of why I love working on the land through the seasons. We have a duty to hand on the land in good condition at the end of our life, and we need people to buy the things we produce and support our efforts. We are looking to make a living from our land, but most of us love doing so in ways that result in barn owls ghosting above the meadows, otters swimming in the becks, and roe deer grazing in the meadows.

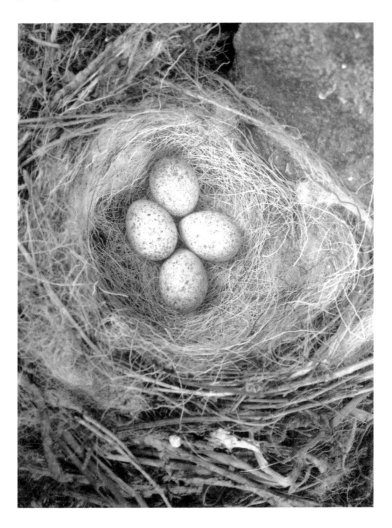

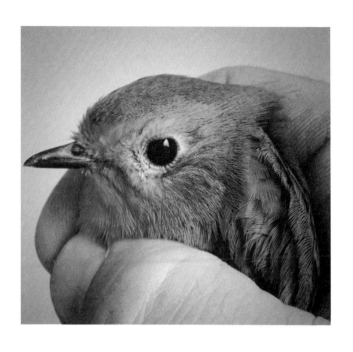

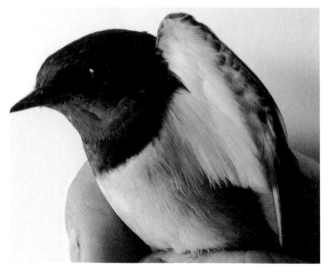

A SHEPHERD'S BUCKET LIST

1. SHEAR IN AN AUSTRALIAN SHEARING SHED

If you are serious about shearing, then you have to test yourself against the best, and some of the best shearers work in the Australian shearing sheds. I went there when I was twenty and wrapped wool. I never got a chance to clip, and now wish I had.

2. FOLLOW THE ST. KILDANS UP THE STACS WITH SHEEP AT ST. KILDA

The Scottish island of St. Kilda is such a strange, isolated place that it is hard to believe that people ever lived there. Even harder to believe is that they sailed four miles across dangerous seas each spring and took sheep to the rocky "stacs" that roar up out of the ocean, and carried the sheep up the cliff faces to the grazing on the stacs' tops and sides. They say the St. Kildans could descend the cliffs in the autumn with a sheep under each arm, down rocky precipices that I would be scared to climb with two free hands. Some of those sheep are still there, a forgotten flock that gets lashed by the Atlantic storms nearly a century after the community left the islands. Part of me would like to re-create that epic shepherding feat; part of me thinks, Maybe not.

3. WALK THROUGH THE DESERT IN RAJASTHAN WITH THE NOMADIC SHEPHERDS

Apparently shepherds in Rajasthan, India, get their own special style and colour of turban to let everyone know their occupation. I went once, and I loved seeing the shepherds trading at the edge of the towns or walking back to the dusty, scrublike desert with their sheep. I started seeing shepherds' red turbans everywhere.

4. WALK A FLOCK DOWN THE DROVE ROADS OF THE CAUSSES AND CÉVENNES

The French take their farming history seriously. In 2006 they got the shepherding landscape of Causses and Cévennes listed as a UNESCO World Heritage Site. Someday I'm going to go and walk the flocks to the summer pastures with the shepherds there. The Lake District where we farm may soon become the second shepherding World Heritage Site, which is incredible considering the role of sheep and cattle in human history. I hope the campaign is successful. Some landscapes are important because they are wild, others because they represent people's work over centuries.

5. SPEND THE SUMMER WITH MILKMAIDS IN NORWAY

Spending a summer with Norwegian milkmaids sounds a bit Benny Hill, but it is all quite innocent. A couple of years ago, I was lucky enough to travel to the valleys of Norway, and I met a shepherd who milked goats and made amazing cheese with their milk. He took me up a long winding track for miles and miles, past dozens of waterfalls, to the traditional summer pastures where his goats grazed. When we got there, it was as though I'd travelled back in time: at the head of the valley were the traditional summerhouses of every family in the village, small wooden houses with bunk beds, and boxes over the streams that work to chill the milk and cheese. Most of the families had stopped taking their flocks to the mountains but had kept their summerhouses. And we met two milkmaids who were spending the summer in the mountains, milking goats. They hadn't seen anyone for days, and came and sat with us to talk. I had to pinch myself to remember that this was the twenty-first century.

6. CAUSE TROUBLE WITH SHEEP IN CENTRAL MADRID

A handful of shepherds made the front page of newspapers all around the world in 2011 when they walked thousands of sheep into central Madrid. They were protesting the fact that their ancient grazing, migration, and droving rights were being destroyed by modern life. There are seventy-eight thousand miles of droving roads in Spain, leading from summer to winter grazing lands. The "shepherds council" they are part of was established in 1273, when Madrid was a little village on a droving route. My favourite detail of the story was that the shepherds knew their legal rights. The head shepherd walked into the town hall and formally paid the correct fee of twenty-five maravedis (maravedis are eleventh-century coins) to a baffled civil servant. The photos showed that the urban residents of Madrid flocked (pardon the pun) in their thousands, with smiling faces, to see this magical pastoral protest take place in their modern city.

7. HERD REINDEER WITH THE SAMI PEOPLE

I love watching people do things in ancient ways, particularly if those things relate to my life at home. Someday I am going to visit the reindeer herders of the far north to learn more about what they do. I don't fancy the extreme cold much, or the truly nomadic lifestyle of some of them, but I suspect from what I have read that it might be like visiting long-lost relatives. I want to hear their reindeer-calling shouts to see if we call the same strange things to our livestock.

8. WALK SHEEP DOWN THE WINDY ALPINE PASSES

One day I will walk one of those flocks down from the mountains with those old shepherds, if they'll have my help. But Floss and Tan will need their passports.

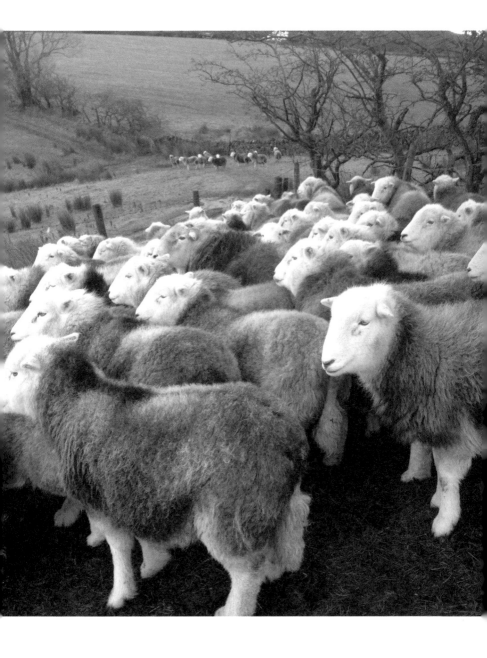

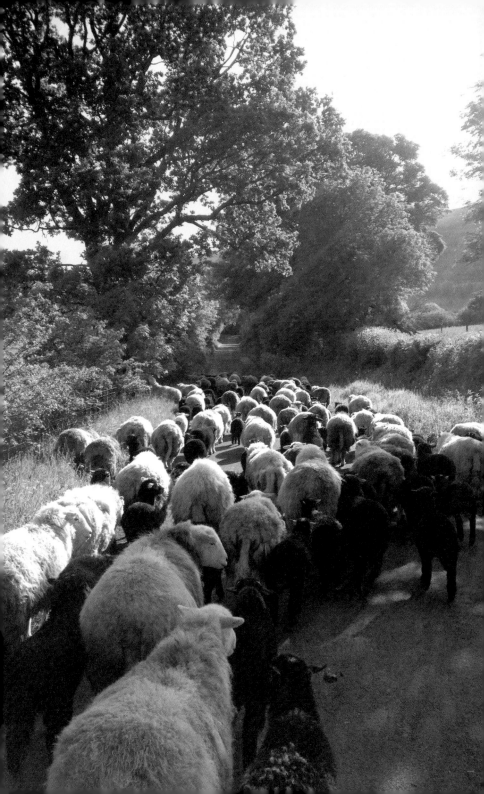

WHY I LOVE MATTERDALE

IT DOESN'T CHANGE MUCH

Change is, of course, good sometimes, but most of us aren't taking any chances.

FATED LOVE

My wife and I thought we chose each other. Our grandmothers, who were great friends, used to smile as if to say that was a charming and naïve interpretation of what really happened. We now think we might have been set up.

PEOPLE SAY WHAT THEY REALLY MEAN

I was rather shocked to discover "small talk" when I left this area in my twenties. A typical conversation here starts with something like:

"What time do you call this?"

"Did you lie in, you lazy sod?"

CREATIVE SWEARING

No one swears with such creativity and venom as Cumbrians. Best friends tear each other apart, with every other word an F or a C. I once heard a man who had been bettered in a sheep deal say, "They say you meet a sharper man round every corner. Well, if you ask me, it would be a fucking lang corner before you met someone sharper than him."

NOBODY IS GOING TO GET TOO BIG FOR THEIR BOOTS

I was recently lucky enough to have some success with a book I wrote called *The Shepherd's Life*. My neighbour rang me up one night and left a message on the answering machine: "It's all very well being a writer and being on the TV and all that stuff, but could you maybe remember to shut your gates, you dopey bugger, because your bloody sheep are on the road. Good night."

THERE ARE MORE SHEEP THAN PEOPLE

Actually, quite a lot more sheep than people. If you are a shepherd, that is good news.

IT IS A LONG WAY FROM LONDON

This is traditionally thought of as a disadvantage, but we see England the other way up, with London as fairly peripheral. We rather delight in being a long way from the capital. Shepherds who have travelled on the Tube generally consider it below the legal welfare standards for transporting sheep. So Shap Fell is considered the southern boundary of our civilization, and passing south of it is only for the brave, the mercenary, or the foolish.

EVERYONE KNOWS YOUR BUSINESS

This can be a pain in the arse, of course, but it saves a lot of small talk. And the jungle drums are very efficient: gossip can pass through the valleys in a matter of an hour or two. Though it can be like Chinese whispers, and what reaches the western valleys of the Lake District is not always the truth that left Matterdale.

MATTERDALE SOCIAL CLUB

We used to have a caravan that doubled as a bait cabin next to our sheep pens. It looked as if it had been stolen from the set of an Eminem video, and was far from luxurious. It had a gas heater for us to get warmed up and an inch of flies on the windowsills. Eating in it was high risk because my dad washed the pots and pans. But despite all of this it became known as "Matterdale Social Club," an unofficial café for every waif and stray person in the valley. When it got smashed to pieces by a storm, we all felt a little sad.

IT IS PARADISE

Even on the worst day of winter I wouldn't want to be anywhere else. When all the joking is said and done, I think it is one of the most wonderful places on earth.

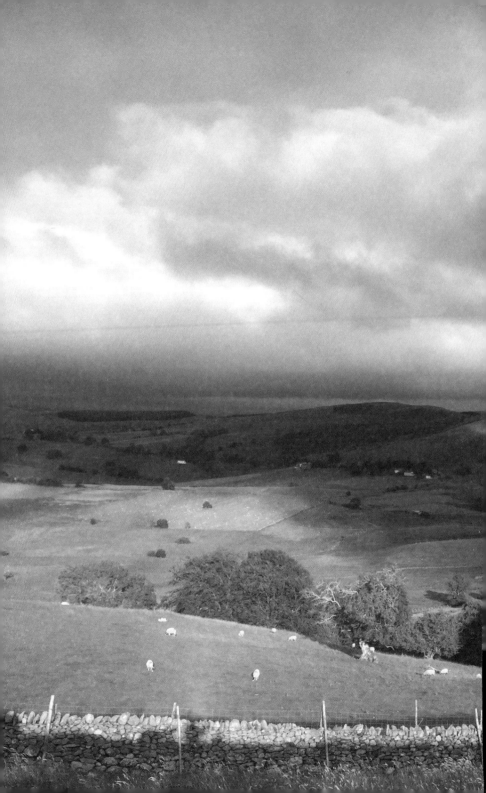

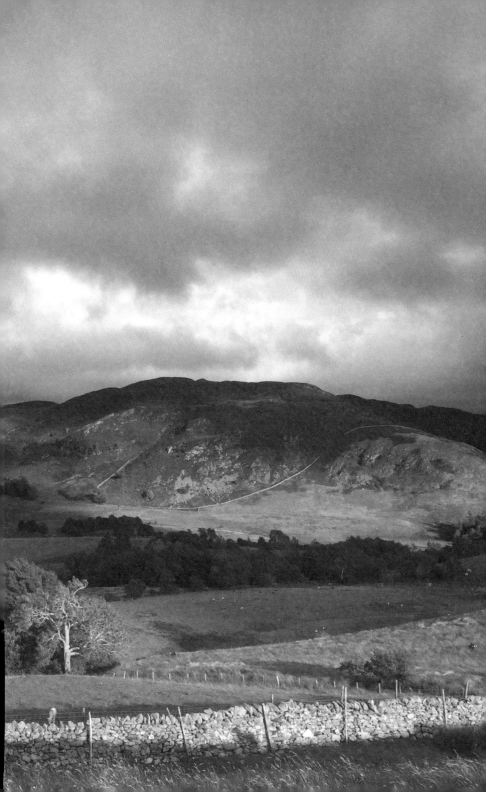

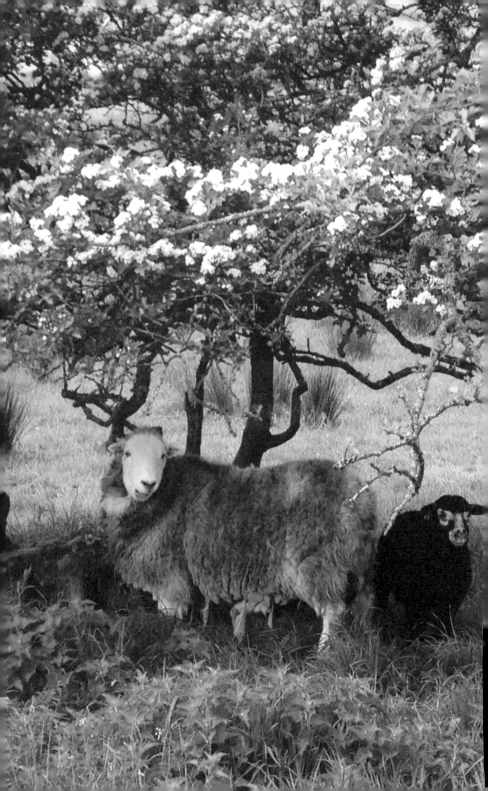

As I drive along the valley bottom, a mist of
shadows and gossamer lies across the fell.

Fields are carved apart with shadows.
Cattle stand on a mound by the roadside,
hairy and sunlit around a feeder. The
sheep graze in green fields and a buzzard
hangs above the woods, catching the sun
like a kite. The rooks glean the stubble
at the edge of the woods.

And maybe someday you'll pass this way
and think it beautiful, too.

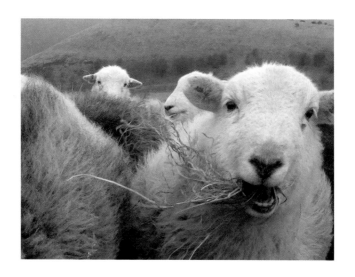

Acknowledgements

To those who follow my working life online and have asked for this book: thank you. I hope you like it.

To Joe, William, Robert, Derek, and Jean: thank you for letting me be cheeky about you.

And finally: thank you to my family, who back me all the way.

About the Author

JAMES REBANKS runs a family-owned farm in the Lake District in northern England. His first book, *The Shepherd's Life*, was a *New York Times* bestseller and named a Top Ten Book of the Year by Michiko Kakutani. He uses his popular Twitter feed (@herdyshepherd1) to share updates on the shepherding year.

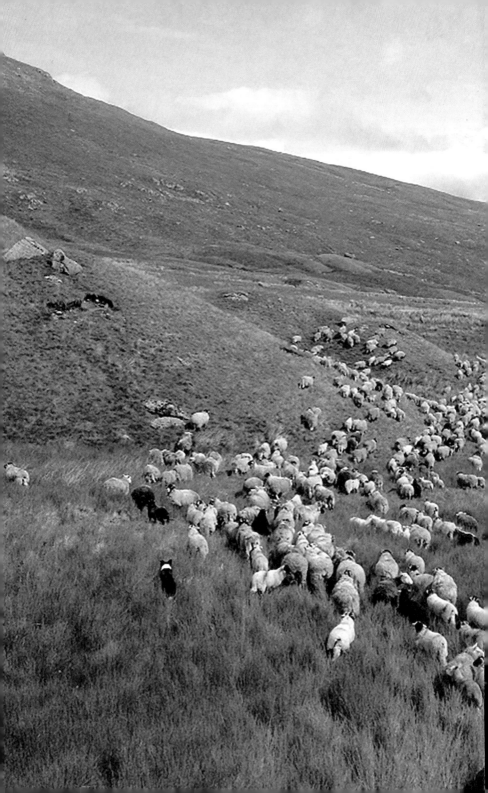